ARCTIC OCEAN

SIBERIA
U.S.S.R.

ALASKA

CANADA

PACIFIC OCEAN

UNITED STATES

JAPAN

HAWAII

MEXICO

ARCTIC CIRCLE

Scale of miles

0   50   100   200

YUKON R.

Dawson

KLONDIKE R.

C

TANANA R.

ALASKA
RANGE

Northway

A

K

A

N

A

WRANGELL RANGE

Whitehorse

Watson Lak

UGACH RANGE

D

Valdez

MT. LOGAN

White Pass

A

MT. ST. ELIAS

Haines

PACIFIC

OCEAN

Sitka

Follow the North Star

Follow the North Star

by TAY THOMAS

1960

Doubleday & Company, Inc., Garden City, N.Y.

TO DAVID LOWELL

*in hopes that he will be
the fourth member of our
next expedition*

CONTENTS

I How Would You Like to Go to Alaska, Dear?   9

II Bye-Bye, Mama   20

III A Guy Named Joe   42

IV The Movie Stars Quit and Turn Tourist   49

V Runaway Glaciers and a Sea of Ice   63

VI Anchorage and the Statehood Celebration

VII We Visit a Farmer in Matanuska Valley   86

VIII Other Alaskan Inhabitants — and a Bush Pilot with a Unique Invention   93

IX McKinley Park — A Luxury Hotel and a Wilderness Camp   103

X On to Fairbanks, the Golden Heart of the North   121

XI North of the Arctic Circle   140

Follow the North Star

CHAPTER I

How Would You Like to Go
to Alaska, Dear?

THE 6:42 express was just pulling in. The station area was jammed with waiting cars; horns honking, wives waving, children calling "Daddy," and the inevitable "Taxi." Men streamed off the platform and cars moved away just as rapidly. Lowell jumped into our front seat, only to be overwhelmed by the greetings of the two children and dog in the rear. A kiss from me and a "how was your day, dear?" were followed by an unusually long silence.

"How would you like to go to Alaska, dear?" he replied.

"Oh sure, I'd love it, and then to Russia, too," I smiled.

"But I'm not kidding — I have to go in three weeks and thought you'd like to go along."

I felt a great jolt. Despite the fact that we were a traveling family and liked to pack up at the drop of a hat, well, this was just too much of a drop!

A few months earlier, Lowell's father had asked him for

a list of places that might be visited during the next year's "High Adventure" television series. Lowell had included Alaska, partly because he could visit it in his own little plane. (Flying is his greatest love in life, my constant competition.) I had not taken him seriously at the time — to tackle those awesome mountains and that frightful weather in our single-engine Cessna 180 seemed sheer suicide to me. Anyway, the idea seemed to disappear beneath a deluge of other grandiose projects. I breathed a sigh of relief and tried to resign myself to the day when I'd have to leave the children for a while — perhaps to drive leisurely through Europe or to loll on the sands of a South Sea isle. Then, somehow, one by one all the glamorous projects fell through and now it was up to Lowell to conquer Alaska with *Charlie* (our airplane) — to produce and write a television story on our future forty-ninth state.

I had to return to everyday living just long enough to drive home, feed the two children, and put them to bed. Then I sat down to tackle the future. Obviously I had to go along — come what may among those mountains and howling snowstorms. We had been through so much together already — flying *Charlie* over the jungles and deserts of Africa, and over some of the wildest country in the world in the Middle East. But that was before we had any children, when life had been an uncomplicated lark.

In fact, I had grown up in a world of aviation, in a life of constant travel and "spur of the moment" changes of plan. My father believed strongly in individualism, and we were constantly being told not to feel or do like others, but to buck the tide and be different. So, while the other children were going to dancing school (Dad's pet aversion), Boy Scout meetings, and country-club swimming classes, my three brothers, my sister, and I spent hours at the local seaplane base, flying in the little Cubs and Stinsons or just plain listening to talk on aviation. My three brothers soloed before they were fifteen, but, although I learned a good deal, because I was the girl, I was relegated to the co-pilot's seat. (I'm just as glad now — I find it altogether too easy to be a back-seat pilot, even with no license to back it all up.)

When we weren't flying in planes, we were all riding on small motorcycles, the whole family racing about on back country roads, ever mindful of the fact that we had to avoid main streets and policemen because we kids were far too young for licenses.

Another of Dad's training programs was designed to toughen us up for future trips to Africa, or other out-of-the-way areas. We often slept out overnight in tents or hammocks, while Dad prowled around us, shooting off shotguns or growling like a lion. I can still feel the pellets raining down on me as I raced toward the house, not caring whether I "flunked" or not. (I was always considered the sissy of the family. I'm sure they thought I was destined to be a stay-at-home housewife, my travels leading me no farther than the local supermarket.)

We spent many winters in Florida, but not lolling on the beach or going to the usual teen-age parties. Instead, we went on great "expeditions" into the Everglades, inevitably managing to bog the car down in a swollen creek or mudhole, leaving us a four- or five-mile hike back to the nearest telephone. Mother knew from long experience to wait until sundown before sending out a search party.

As we grew older, this became the perfect way for Dad and my brothers to test any of my unsuspecting boy friends. I will never forget one "beau" who "joined the expedition," wearing white ducks and a pith helmet. The boys immediately marked down ten points against him, but when he dramatically leaped from our truck to shoot a baby alligator with his Abercrombie rifle, his goose was cooked. So was mine, after the seven-mile walk home that night.

As we grew older, we began to take longer trips, to Canada, Central and South America, and Africa. (How convenient that Dad worked for Pan American World Airways and we all could fly free!) One brother spent a summer vacation in the Belgian Congo. Dad had given him $200 (and his airline pass) for the entire trip. Tap came home with $300 and the explanation that he had gotten into a crap game with some Pan American pilots.

About this time I began to wonder if I would ever find a husband whose way of life was similar to mine. I went on to Smith College (one of my more normal experiences), majoring in geography (what else?), and I will never be remembered there for marks nor campus activities, just for taking a long weekend during my senior year in order to visit Hawaii. That, too, was the year I met Lowell, and, needless to say, it didn't take us long to find out how much we had in common. I had no worries about parental or fraternal approval, though my brothers still tease Lowell that he was marrying for a Pan Am pass, which I lost the moment I became independent. (He did seem quite indignant — I wonder?)

The next five years were ones of constant travel for us, at first all over the world on the more conventional airlines and then with our single-engine Cessna. While some people thought we were courageous and others knew we were crazy, I really never gave our flying exploits much thought. We were young, and together, with no little ones dependent upon us back home.

Now, faced with our first expedition since the births of both children, another flying trip in *Charlie* over wild terrain,

I was just plain scared to death. Four years of aging contributed — I was the wiser for our past close calls. But what would become of the children? I thought now. For the next few days my thoughts were in a turmoil. I just couldn't become a stay-at-home wife. I had to face the flight, but it might be easier if I took one child along. Why not take Anne? David was not a year old yet and obviously would not miss us too much. But Anne was two and a half now, Mommy and Daddy were all-important to her, and she was a great joy to both of us. Wouldn't she be happier going along with us, regardless of the travel and living conditions involved? But high-strung, super-energetic Anne could barely sit still in a car long enough to drive two hours to visit her grandparents, much less take a five-hour non-stop flight in *Charlie*'s small back seat. This thought was equally frightening, almost enough to deter me, but not quite. It just had to work.

The big problem now was to convince Lowell, and I had to wait for the most appropriate moment before I gently broached such a difficult subject. Of course he was appalled at the very idea. But when I carefully pointed out what an advantage she would be to the television film he would be making and promised that if we interfered with his work in any way we would immediately return home, he finally acquiesced. (I did not mention my dilemma over leaving children behind — men just don't seem to appreciate such thoughts.) But I think that he, too, really hated the idea of leaving his blue-eyed, dark-haired flirtatious daughter.

Now the preparations began in earnest. (One of the three weeks of valuable time had already slipped by.) A home had to be found for David (what would we do without grandmothers?). And another for Boaz, our oversized German shepherd. Next to *Charlie*, Bozie is Lowell's greatest joy in life. Thank heaven he isn't the size of a dachshund, or Lowell would have insisted that he come with us. Anne and *Charlie* had checkups, at the doctor's and airport shop respectively. Neither of them presented us with any trouble, although the airplane was outfitted with a new set of oversized tires, good for rough sand or gravel airstrips. The same VHF and HF radios we had used overseas would be fine for Alaska. The instruments were all still in good shape, but we had to make a new copy of our favorite poem which had been taped on the instrument panel all during our world flight:

> *Peace be in thy home*
> *And in thy heart,*
> *Or if thou roam*
> *Earth's highways wide,*
> *The Lord be at thy side*
> *To bless and guide.*
>
> (R. E. CLEEVE)

We also had to buy stacks of new aeronautical maps and large planning charts, enough to cover our entire route from New Jersey to Alaska and all the areas we might conceivably fly over while there. Most of our evenings were spent on the living-room floor, maps spread out around us. Distances and hours of flying had to be carefully computed. Where would we refuel and spend the nights? What were the towns where we could tackle American and Canadian customs?

The answer to the last question, and to many others, we found in the Alaska Flight Information Manual, a handbook published for fliers by the Civil Aeronautics Administration. We spent many hours studying the vital information in it — the list of radio frequencies, weather broadcast schedules, detailed airport information, and flight-plan procedure. I was greatly reassured to read that pilots are always urged to file a flight plan, that the Search and Rescue Organization in Alaska is a highly efficient and successful operation. Then I was appalled to see the sentence which followed: "FAILURE TO FILE A FLIGHT PLAN ALSO MAY RESULT IN IN-FLIGHT IDENTIFICATION BY FIGHTER AIRCRAFT." Many would be the flights when I had that creepy feeling that something was following us — an F–89 or 102 on *Charlie*'s tail.

We were both amazed to read the Canadian requirements for single-engine aircraft flying along the Alaska Highway. A two-way radio, pocket compass, camp ax, mosquito netting, and matches were all understandable, but "snare wire (four ounces), one small gill net, fishing tackle, red flares, signaling mirror, and firearms" made us really wonder what we were getting into.

The problem of what clothing to take was my biggest headache, especially because *Charlie*'s small size limited us to one suitcase apiece. I pestered Lowell for details about Alaskan weather (he had been there twice before), but he, being a typical male, with little or no interest in clothes, gave me the most non-committal replies.

"Oh, it's like around here in the spring — it can get hot in some places and cold in others." Kind of tough requirements for one suitcase. To further complicate the situation, we had to keep in mind the type of clothing which was best suited for color and black-and-white photography. Add the usual laundry headaches to this complex problem, and I had an impossible situation.

I finally packed my suitcase with a wool suit and coat, wool slacks and skirt, several drip-dry cottons, blue jeans, and as many sweaters as I could squeeze in. (My guess later turned out to be quite accurate, although the cottons never made it back home after constant heavy wear.) I also added a bathing suit in a kind of hopeful gesture — a bit of wishful thinking. (What a laugh, I thought.)

I decided Anne's wardrobe would be a good deal simpler — just dress her in her usual corduroy pants and blouses most of the time. Here's where I made my first big mistake. We had barely reached Ohio when Anne rebelled. She was a big girl going on a big trip now and therefore would always have to wear dresses. I gave in and bought four pretty cotton ones in Minnesota, thereby adding considerably to my laundry burden. But I was a lucky laundress in that Anne was out of the diaper stage — in the daytime anyway. The one or two at night were no problem, far better than leaving a string of wet hotel beds or ruined sleeping bags behind us.

We sent ski apparel on ahead of us to Juneau in a duffle bag. We would need these winter clothes only for our visit to the Juneau Icecap. I had a hard time finding this type of clothing small enough to fit Anne, but finally bought a frightfully expensive pair of "stretch" ski pants, figuring they would stretch enough to fit her for the next two winters, then David for another two after that.

Once the clothing problem was more or less under control, the next hurdle was what to take to keep Anne amused during the long plane rides and sieges of hotel living. Obviously her favorite tricycle and baby carriage had to be left behind. Also, innumerable dolls, housekeeping equipment, and even heavy books. But in one of my many "what to do" moments, I had a veritable brainstorm — why not take her miniature portable victrola which she played from the moment she woke up until she went to bed at night. This would be the perfect solution for hotel rooms and well worth the small addition to luggage.

And, of course, "Fooey," her well-worn rabbit, had to go along — he became an important member of the expedition. It might be calamitous to Lowell to lose a piece of equipment somewhere, but if we ever misplaced "Fooey" we might just as well have headed for home. The essentials for the airplane included comic books (she had just discovered how interesting they were, and they weighed less than books), crayons, and a few miniature toys kept in what I called the "emergency box" — for those moments of sheer desperation.

All these diversions, except the victrola, fit into a handy little plaid satchel which I pinned to the back of my seat while we were flying. In the pocket behind Lowell's seat I kept a secret supply of chewing gum, life-savers, and lollipops, also for emergency. On the back shelf reposed a large box of Kleenex, a sickness container (never used), and a unique little waterproof cardboard potty. This turned out to be about the most important item in the entire airplane. Anne usually made her announcement just when we were high over the wildest territory, miles from the nearest airfield.

The other most important item which we squeezed into an already crowded cabin was another plaid satchel containing a small electric heating unit, the size of a large tumbler (advertised as good for heating water for coffee), two plastic coffee cups and saucers and spoons. The heater had two electrical plugs — one we could use in all hotel rooms and the other to fit into the cigarette lighter on our airplane dashboard. While flying along at 8000 feet I could make hot cups of bouillon! The soup and coffee helped greatly to break the monotony of a long flight, but I had to pick my cooking time carefully — boiling water spilled on my lap because of an air bump was not my idea of fun.

Best of all, though, was that with the small heating unit

I could cook entire meals for Anne in the hotels where the dining hours were often too late for her. Rice, spaghetti, vegetables, and soups could all be cooked in that way. What a great boon that unit was — a must when traveling with young children.

Now we had used up all the room in the cabin, but we found big spaces beneath the seats, which we stuffed with our emergency food supply (Canadian law requires light planes flying the Alaska Highway to carry food for three days): rice, chocolate, dehydrated soups, raisins, a few tins of meat and cheese, two canteens of water, and indispensable packages of powdered milk. Anne was a big milk drinker and we knew fresh milk would be a problem while traveling and in the more isolated areas. I conducted an intense psychological campaign at home to win her over to the powdered product. The result was a complete fiasco, and I worried a good deal about it. How silly I was! The first night we camped out, Lowell filled Anne's favorite bedtime bottle with cold mountain-stream water, added the powdered milk, gave it a few shakes, and handed it to her. She went to bed with it and drank it down without a murmur. From then on she consumed gallons of the powdered stuff, and Mommy made mental notes to throw out some of her psychological ideas.

In the little baggage compartment, above and around the suitcases, we wedged in mosquito head nets, two mess kits, a small primus stove, sleeping bags, and two still cameras. Amazing what those Cessnas can carry! It was not so much a problem of weight this time (on our African jaunt we flew with a two-hundred-pound overload), it was a question of space.

Now all that remained was the inevitable round of parties and visits with friends and family. I always have morbid feelings about these gatherings — imagining a general attitude of "those crazy Thomases are at it again" and "their luck is bound to run out on this one." Only this time I wasn't just imagining such thoughts. Our families were horrified that we were subjecting "poor baby Anne" to such expedition rigors. Friends were horrified that we were subjecting ourselves to the tribulations of travel with a two-year-old brat. And everyone shook heads, with wordless frowns, when we announced our method of transportation. "That little airplane over all that ice and snow ―――――― " (I privately agreed 100 per cent. At least I wasn't alone in my fears, but I would sure be alone with them in *Charlie*.) It was surprising to us how many people still thought of Alaska as a land of igloos, Eskimos, and polar bears. Anne came in for her share of morale building, too. It seemed inevitable that some well-meaning soul would lean down, greeting her with a "poor dear" smile and "what a lucky girl, going to see all those big white bears." By the time we were ready to leave, Anne was convinced that Alaska's only inhabitants were those monstrous animals, and she was very leery of going near the place at all. And I must admit that there were many moments when I felt exactly the same way.

CHAPTER II

Bye-Bye, Mama

SATURDAY, May 17th, dawned gray and murky, a much appreciated bon voyage present from the weather man. Anne and I had gone to Connecticut to leave David with his grandparents. Lowell was to pick us up at the Westchester County Airport at 9:00 A.M. At ten o'clock we still couldn't see Long Island Sound a half mile beyond my family's house. So we spent the rest of the morning just waiting for the weather to clear. Anne, dressed in her travel clothes, went down to the beach and returned looking more like a bundle of old rags washed up by the tide than a traveler just about to set off on a big trip.

At noon we finally headed for the airport — the whole family, friends of mine, friends of Anne's: confusion and chaos all combined to make an unforgettable departure. Lowell landed shortly thereafter, with a bare two miles' visibility. *Charlie* was looking sleek and trim, his black, red, and white paint job jaunty and shiny, the colorful flags along his sides a tribute to all the countries he had already con-

quered. We said hasty good-bys, partly because I was finding it harder than I had thought to leave David. When he
said, "Bye-Bye, Mama," practically the first words he had
ever uttered, I almost couldn't make it into the airplane.
I could barely squeeze in anyway, despite our careful planning. We even had to do some last-minute shifting around
to free the back seat for Anne. Finally, with the picnic
luncheon on my lap, my oversized handbag wedged beneath my feet, and "Fooey" stuffed into the space between
our seats, we were ready to try closing the door. We called
good-bys again, and my father yelled some last-minute
parental advice: "Remember, if you get caught in a thunderstorm, throw your baggage out first!" Pondering on those
cheerful words as we taxied toward the runway, I wondered
what he meant for us to throw out second. And if Lowell had
any plans to fly even within ten miles of any thunderstorm,
I would be "second," but I'd jump out right now!

Before I could think further, we were off into the still
thick haze. Within a few moments we had climbed above
it and found clear blue sky. My spirits revived, especially
when I glanced toward the back seat to find Anne asleep
before we had even leveled off.

At 8000 feet, we sped over New Jersey. Homing on
Phillipsburg radio, we crossed the Pennsylvania state line,
on over the Appalachian Mountains in unusually clear
weather until we finally let down and landed at Akron, Ohio,
at 4:00 P.M. Lowell would have liked to continue on to
Chicago, but I felt we shouldn't push Anne the first day,
especially after such a late start.

By the end of our second day of flying, it had finally
dawned on us that the United States is a very large country.
Two days of hours and hours of flying, and there we were
in Madison, Wisconsin, barely out of the East. We did have

terrible head winds of thirty to forty miles per hour, which reduced our ground speed to 115 miles per hour, little better than driving.

At noon on the third day we came down at Minneapolis for gas and lunch. The wind was still gusting up to forty miles per hour, so we tied *Charlie* down before going into the terminal for some lunch. Anne was holding up beautifully, sleeping most of the time in *Charlie* and thoroughly enjoying the many hamburgers and milk shakes at all our stops. Lowell and I were just beginning to relax and enjoy ourselves.

Then disaster struck. We returned to the hangar and while Anne and I went to the rest room, and Lowell stopped to pay for the gas, an attendant headed for the airplane. By the time we had started for it, he was coming back, and then we realized that he had completely untied it and removed the chocks — in a forty-mile-an-hour wind! We saw the first strong gust start to blow *Charlie* toward a Seabee about twenty-five feet away. We raced toward him frantically, and Lowell got there just as *Charlie*'s wing hit the Seabee. He was able to push the tail away and deflect the blow a little, and the attendant and I arrived a moment later to push the plane back where it belonged.

We were so upset we couldn't say anything at first and dreaded looking over the damage. We were afraid the whole wing had been damaged, and Lowell only said tersely, "There's the end of our trip." But when we looked *Charlie* all over carefully, it seemed that only the aileron had been crumpled. We pushed the plane into the hangar, and the mechanics there quickly confirmed our new fears — no spare ailerons in the vicinity. It would take three days to get another from the Cessna plant in Wichita. Lowell grumbled that it had taken just as long for us to receive a spare part in the Belgian Congo and headed for the telephone. Within ten minutes the local Cessna distributor received instructions to borrow the part from a new plane, so within two hours *Charlie* was ready to fly again — but it was too late to continue that day. I was secretly immensely glad because the wind was blowing even harder by then, and also my two college roommates lived in Minneapolis and here was my chance for our first visit since graduation in 1949.

Tuesday, May 20th, was a long hard day of flying, to try to make up for lost time. And despite the pilot's apparent loss of memory, it was also our eighth wedding anniversary. No party, or dancing, or a show this evening. Back home, Lowell might have suggested a movie. We had planned to fly all the way to Great Falls, Montana, that day, our jumping-off point for Canada, but the going was unusually slow and extremely rough. Over the Dakota Badlands we were tossed and bounced about. The rugged desertlike country beneath us became hilly, adding considerably to the turbulence. I finally persuaded Lowell to stop short of Great Falls, at Lewiston, a little town virtually hidden by its magnificent surroundings — snow-capped mountains, dark pine tree-covered hills, and rolling green pastureland. The pilot grumbled that we probably wouldn't even find a hotel in such a spot, but the co-pilot was desperate enough to use the sleeping bags. Seven hours is a long time just to sit and bounce about.

The size of the airfield was all out of proportion to the town — a large old World War II bomber training base that looked like a ghost field now. One hangar still appeared to be occupied, sheltering four crop-dusting planes. A weather-beaten westerner, complete with blue jeans and sombrero, sauntered out to give us gas and obligingly called up the local taxi, a prewar vintage Ford with a large sign, "McGlinty For Sheriff," on top.

The town itself was a very pleasant surprise — an extremely attractive one, with quiet, shade-tree-lined streets, well-kept lawns, and neat frame houses. And there was a hotel, small but comfortable. In fact, it seemed more like a home, especially since we never saw another guest. There was no dining room nor convenient local restaurant, though, so while Anne watched television with the hotel proprietors, and I did my nightly laundry, Lowell walked to the local supermarket. Within an hour we had a feast fit for an anniversary right in our own room — cold cuts, carrots, tomatoes, cucumbers, soup cooked in our electric cooker, and a glass of California wine for a toast. To many more years of smooth flying together!

The next morning we were off on an uneventful flight due north over Montana and across the Canadian border to Edmonton. (The first border I have ever crossed that was actually marked! A fence stretched straight out below us as far as we could see.) The country was flat farmland, but far to the left we could see the snow-covered Rockies, an unbroken line all along our course. We found Edmonton, the capital of Alberta, to be another big city like Minneapolis or Akron (a population of over 230,000), with the usual luxurious hotels, but just ahead of us lay the real beginning of the most exciting part of our flight to Alaska — following the Alaska Highway up through the wilderness of British Columbia and the Yukon Territory to the Alaskan border.

It was in Edmonton that we joined forces with a young Alaskan bush pilot, Merrill Wien. His Cessna 180 would accompany ours, carrying our director, Jean Philippe Carson, and cameraman, Mike Murphy. To me the word "bush pilot" was the epitome of daring, spectacular flying feats in the wilds, so I wasn't quite sure whether to greet Merrill as friend or foe. (I could clearly envision the day when I'd be begging

Lowell not to tackle a frightening flying situation, while Merrill was confidently urging him on.)

And foremost in my mind was a tale of horror which Lowell had related to me — about a bush pilot, of course. It was a day filled with close calls in a 1930 vintage Stinson on floats, with a devil-may-care, "seat-of-the-pants" pilot at the controls. Their first take-off set the mood for the day. The lake was actually two, connected by an artificial channel. The distance from the end of one to the end of the other was less than a mile. The pilot started at full throttle, (fifty miles an hour) down one lake and through the channel. Lowell waited for take-off at any moment, but the old crate was still stuck to the water when they reached the end lake. The pilot then swung to the right and began a "hair-raising" (Lowell's own words — that's important because I usually use the word "hair-raising" for some event he doesn't even consider worth mentioning) step turn to the left, still at full throttle. Everything would have worked out fine if a swimming float hadn't suddenly loomed up directly in front of them. They missed it by inches and headed back into the channel again, still glued to the glassy water. Lowell said, "My nerves had just about had it, and I was ready to open the door and dive out, not a bad idea at our slow rate of speed."

About halfway back down the channel again, the pilot horsed the plane up on one float, the right wing tip just a few feet from the water, then hauled back on the wheel, yanking the old crate off the water. They staggered into the air, barely clearing the hangars at the far end of the farthest lake. "Jeez, what a way to go!" was the only comment from the pilot, and one which Lowell heard many more times throughout his day of horror.

The next crisis came within an hour of take-off. They

had been drawing gas from both tanks, but one suddenly read empty and the other full. "Holy Josephine! That just ain't so!" from the pilot. A large red streak over the wing indicated they were losing precious fuel — they had lost a breather stem from the left gas cap, leaving a hole. The change in pressure caused the gas in the good tank to "cross-feed" into the other, where the wind simply siphoned it out through that hole. A disastrous way to use up one's precious gas supply.

They swooped down onto the nearest lake (it was labeled Sucker Lake on the map, making Lowell wonder just who was the sucker) and before long were off again, with an ingenious wooden plug and piece of pipe patching up the hole. "Holy Josephine!" Then "Jeez, what a way to go!"

Another hour of staggering through the air brought them to a wilderness lake where they had a rendezvous with a red and silver Beaver which had brought them tins of gas. (The Stinson's fuel capacity was two hours!) Checking the oil, the pilot found the level didn't even show on the dip stick! And after only one and a half hours of flight! "Oh man, what a thirsty engine. A fellow would have to be a millionaire to keep this baby full of gas and oil." So saying, he reached into the rear of the plane for two quarts of oil. "Jeez, what a way to go!"

After another harrowing take-off (using up two miles of lake water), they flew on west to a hazardous mountain pass, the Beaver right behind them. They soon became lost and headed up the wrong canyon. (Of course the plane had no compass.) The pilot began looking more and more at the map, and less and less out the window. Lowell watched a rapidly approaching steep rock wall. He finally tapped the pilot on the shoulder. "Holy Josephine!" as he rolled the plane into a steep 180 degrees, and then the inevitable "Jeez, what a way to go!" The Beaver had prudently waited at the entrance to the dead end. After an hour more of flying, and another stop for gas and oil, they finally found the mountain pass. Once the photography was completed (the purpose of this day of horror), both the Beaver and the Stinson headed home. "Then," said Lowell, "we had the fright of our lives, and after all that we had just been through —" The pilot had relaxed for a moment and was eating some fried chicken. Lowell was sitting absent-mindedly, staring at the instrument panel. Suddenly some movement in the left window caught Lowell's eye. It was red and silver, and so close that the window was filled with it. The Beaver! Lowell quickly hooked two fingers around the pilot's wheel and yanked back. This brought his companion to with a start, and he now hauled back, too. The Beaver slid by under their nose, not missing the propeller by more than twenty-five feet, the other pilot apparently totally unaware of what had come within a hairsbreadth of happening — a mid-air collision. "Jeez, what a way to go!"

So, with this picture of a bush pilot in my mind, I greeted Merrill Wien. I was in for quite a surprise — Merrill completely disarmed me with a warm smile on his extremely handsome face. He was tall and dark-haired — in his airline uniform (his more normal work) he would be a knockout! He was also a bit shy, but good-natured. In short, he could lead us into any flying situation and I was not going to complain! And he obviously knew a great deal about flying. You could say being a bush pilot was his hobby. He had had vast experience in the Air Force, flying multi-engine planes, and was now flying huge airliners (for Wien Alaska, his father's airline) on scheduled runs all over the Arctic.

To complete our party, our director and cameraman flew in to join us the next day. J.P. was a husky six feet four,

with handlebar mustache, incongruous crew cut, and faint
French accent. An infinitely calm person, he never raised
his voice, except when Canadian Customs refused to let
him bring in twenty pounds of his favorite tea and twelve
cartons of French cigarettes. He was allowed to keep his
own teapot, however. Michael Patrick Murphy, all six feet
four of him, was just as calm and easygoing, despite his
name. He was always ready and willing for anything, the
more adventure the better. Often carrying thirty or forty
pounds of equipment for hours on end, or hiking up a steep
mountainside, or working in water up to his waist.

Now all were present and raring to go, so we planned
to take off at nine the following morning. But what a beginning! Complete and utter confusion at the airport from nine
until nearly eleven o'clock. Lowell and I were fairly used to
loading *Charlie* by now — with lots of practice each day away
from New York. Every bag or container, or toy or potty
had its particular place and had to fit just so. If Anne's
suitcase was turned around the wrong way, we lost a half
inch of space and the brief cases wouldn't fit in. Or if we
rolled up one sleeping bag in the wrong way, the rucksack
couldn't possibly fit in. And we knew just which things
we'd need in flight and whether they should be in or out
of Anne's reach. So we stowed away our luggage within ten
minutes' time. The confusion began when J.P. and Mike
deposited all their gear in front of Merrill's plane. The cab
drivers gaped — everyone gaped! We knew Cessnas could
carry a lot, but the mounds of boxes of camera and sound
gear, film supplies, duffle bags, and a huge heavy tripod
looked impossible. Plus the two men who were both six
feet four and a pilot who was a mere six feet one! Two
hours of waiting around for us now (while Anne minutely
examined every plane in the hangars and inveigled two

packs of chewing gum and a Coca-Cola from the mechanics) until they finally got everything in but the tripod. Mike squeezed into one corner of the back seat and held it between his knees.

Lowell took this time to report to the Royal Canadian Air Force for a briefing and clearance to fly on north. (The route between Edmonton and the Alaskan border is a military air route, and so under the jurisdiction of the RCAF.) Lowell was told that the limits for such flights were a minimum ceiling of 2000 feet and five miles of visibility. He was also told about the emergency rations and gear required, and of the refueling stops en route. He then checked the weather and filed a flight plan to Fort Nelson, with a refueling stop at Fort St. John. A long complicated procedure, but most reassuring once we were on our way and could see the vast wilderness beneath us.

Off at eleven o'clock — no place to stop for lunch today — we took sandwiches. The countryside was wilderness: great forests of pine and aspen, the thin white line of the one and only road, and an occasional cultivated field. I wondered about these hardy homesteaders and their small houses so far from even the highway. We also noticed large patches of burned timber along the road, undoubtedly some motorist careless with a cigarette. Our Canadian flier's handbook warns pilots not to toss out cigarettes either. Apparently seventy-five per cent of the butts tossed down from the air remain lit after they land.

The land was hilly now and we noticed a curious thing — dark green pine trees on one slope and light green aspen on the other, with the ridge dividing them like a sharp knife. And always far to our left, the snow-covered Rockies. In order to reach Juneau we had to fly north until we came to the Yukon and its large tributaries, then follow river valleys and gorges west, then south into southeastern Alaska. Of course always following the Alaska Highway — a roundabout route, but no single-engine plane is allowed to cross such high uncharted snow and glaciers.

We landed at Fort St. John, about 415 miles northwest of Edmonton, in British Columbia, at three o'clock, to refuel, one plane coming in right behind the other. The sight of that little yellow Cessna just ahead of us at all times had been quite a comfort over all that wilderness. We had the most unusual ritual just before each landing. Anne was almost always asleep, and I'd reach back to shake her (it's best that anyone be awake while descending, because of change of pressure in ears) and yell, "Wake up and yawn, we're coming down." Invariably she'd open her mouth wide, then go back to sleep, leaving it wide open. That seemed to do the trick, anyway.

Our refueling stop was just a small RCAF station — a few wooden buildings, a hangar, and a control tower in the middle of nowhere. (The village of Fort St. John was nearby, an Indian trading post dating back to 1806.) So we were on our way as soon as possible, with 250 miles to cover to Fort Nelson, where we planned to spend the night. This time we divided up, Merrill following the radio beam (flying direct) while we "flew" the highway, buzzing along just a few hundred feet above it. Anne loved this and gave up sleep in favor of watching the few trucks and cars and the little overnight settlements. We saw one poor man jacking up his car to change a flat tire. "Go by air, Joe!" (We feel that "going by air" via airlines and flying via puddle jumper are two entirely different modes of travel. In a big plane one inevitably has a high-altitude view of a flat, muted landscape or, more frequently, a solid layer of fleecy clouds. When you fly in a little plane, you go lower and slower and are on much more intimate terms with the landscape. Below 2000 feet, swooping low over hills and treetops, we feel we can see as much as, if not more than, in a car.)

We had heard that motorists averaged two flat tires per trip on this gravel highway. But that's the penalty for going too fast, according to an Alaskan guidebook. If a motorist averages forty miles per hour on the 1527-mile highway, he isn't likely to get into any trouble, even in the wintertime, although certain precautionary measures are essential then (engine heaters, chains, sleeping bags, etc.). There are inns and gas stations about every thirty miles along the route and highway patrols for those who do need help. The highway is in its poorest shape during the spring thaws in April and May, and then the summer dust clouds take over, making life miserable for the impatient motorists who find themselves behind a big truck. It takes drivers about a week to cover the whole route from Edmonton to Fairbanks, while we planned to make it to Whitehorse in three easy flying days. (Merrill did it in one when he came down to join us.)

Flying along above this wide gravel road (in many places we could easily have landed on it), in the midst of such a vast wilderness of forests and mountains, deep river gorges and bottomless glacial lakes, we wondered at the feat of building it in the first place. We read later that this great highway, originally called Alcan (short for Alaska and Canada), had been the subject of much controversy, and many condemned such a daring project as a complete waste of money and man power (14,000 men were involved). Private contractors and army engineers began to work on it in April 1942, under the direction of the U. S. Corps of Engineers and the Bureau of Public Roads. Alaska was being threatened by the Japanese then, and it was vital to push through such a transportation link. The road was completed in eight months, a phenomenal achievement in the history of highway engineering. Today thousands of tourists use the road every year, and the trucking and freighting along it will probably increase tremendously in the near future. There's even talk of building a railroad beside it.

We took great pride in beating "93 Delta" to the runway at Fort Nelson, despite our circuitous route, but Merrill was carrying airplane skis above his wheels, which slowed him down at least ten miles per hour. One pull of a lever in his cockpit and he could land on snow or smooth glacial ice. The airfield was the usual small RCAF outpost, and the town (built in 1947 as a highway camp), a few miles away, was a rough, tough frontier town of the first order — dirt highway down the middle of two rows of ramshackle wooden buildings, a number of filling stations, two small hotels, innumerable bars, a little wooden church with weeds up to its doorstep (obviously the door was seldom used), a Hudson's Bay trading-post store, also a tiny shack about the size of its sign, which read "Myrtle's Apparel for Ladies," and a few small cabinlike homes. One had a shiny new red and green swing-slide-seesaw combination sitting on the dirt in front of the house — what a contrast!

There were broken glasses and beer bottles lying on the ground outside our two-storied wooden hotel and a big sign just inside that said, "Please leave your boots downstairs." That eliminated one sleep-disturbing noise, anyway! Our room was a nice large one with two double beds and a bathroom, the latter a real surprise. But our big windows, with flimsy "see-through" curtains, were just above the main entrance, and a prominent red neon HOTEL sign hung just outside. When I commented on this obstacle to slumber, Lowell said, "Oh well, the sun doesn't go down until midnight, so you'll have only a few hours of darkness to worry about!"

Whereupon the men deserted us for one of the many town pubs for cold beer. Anne and I found the local cafeteria (just beneath our room), a third-rate greasy-spoon restaurant, complete with gaudy jukebox and the toughest-looking customers I have ever seen. Road workers, oil drillers, lumberjacks, and maybe a prospector or two — dirty blue jeans, dusty cowboy boots, unshaven, uncut heads with hats on — all villains from a Western! Despite the incessant stares, we enjoyed a good dinner of steak, potatoes, and pasteurized milk. Then back upstairs to get some sleep. The noise outside was even louder than expected, but Anne and I finally dozed off around midnight. Lowell stayed awake listening to a rip-roaring party going on, it seemed, just beneath our windows. He said next morning that it sounded like a riot, with teen-age girls screaming some of the worst language he had ever heard.

When we all staggered down to breakfast in the morning, I talked with the waitress a bit. She confirmed that the town was of the roughest type, that she and her husband and their eighteen-year-old daughter had come there just a few months before to "help run a restaurant in a nice small trading-post town." Now they were in a great hurry to turn around and go home, especially because of the daughter. She, I noticed the evening before, was having a wonderful time flirting with all of the men while waiting on tables.

We were in a great hurry to get out, too, and today would be an exciting day for us (if we could just keep our eyes open) because we planned to land by the highway and camp out overnight. We had been anxious to put all our camping gear to work and also our waitress friend had warned us that our next overnight stop, Watson Lake, was even worse than Fort Nelson. Mosquitoes, bears, emergency rations, hard ground — anything to avoid another experience like the previous night's.

Our flight that day was one of the most thrilling and exciting we have ever experienced. Soon after take-off we were surrounded by snow-covered mountains as far as we could see, and the road we were following wound through deep gorges. Mike and J.P. were following us with the cameras today and time after time, when we had just zoomed through a narrow pass, a few hundred feet above the ground, with mountains towering above us, they would say, "That looks great, but please turn around and do it again." (The theme of the television story was that of a family flying north to Alaska in a single-engine airplane to visit the new forty-ninth state.* *Charlie*, Lowell, Anne, and I were to be among the stars.) But I wasn't enjoying this type of stardom one bit, especially when we came to a spectacular glacial lake of turquoise water, with its ice just breaking up enough to reveal a dazzling reflection of the snow-covered mountains above. We were asked several times to swoop low over this icy bath. I felt the plane was a mere fifty feet from the water and panicked at the thought of crash landing in such a spot. Finally Lowell called to Merrill over the radio: "Am having a mutiny aboard, let's call it quits." I had had ample opportunity to count the hordes of trout lying on the lake bottom.

Just a few miles beyond the lake we found the emergency landing strip (Liard River) which we planned to use in order to camp out. It was well hidden from the road and the river was just a mile away. We could see a large gravel bar from the air, which would be perfect for our tents (and Merrill discovered later that he could land his plane on it, thereby eliminating a large baggage-carrying problem). We

---

* We were gambling on the fact that statehood would come through that summer.

tied *Charlie* down at the edge of the strip, and, with Lowell carrying Anne pig-a-back, we started through the thick underbrush toward the river's edge. Just a few steps along I stumbled on some dried dung and wondered whose cow could be there. Then it suddenly dawned on me that the little round ones belonged to bear and the big flat ones to moose. That was a rude shock, and I rushed to catch up with Lowell, looking over my shoulder all the way. "M-o-o-s-e and b-e-a-r [we were always careful to spell out such words] are timid creatures, aren't they?"

"Oh sure," Lowell shrugged it off. But just how timid can a thousand-pound animal be?

The gravel bar was a fine sand beach, a peninsula jutting out into the river. Anne had a field day, running about in her bare feet, playing in the sand. Fortunately it was an unusually hot day, the temperature in the eighties, and the men even went swimming in the ice-cold water. Then, while they put up our tents, Anne and I went to the river to get water. We were quite certain it was pure, because our map showed no settlement for miles, however, we thought we'd boil it to be on the safe side. But was it muddy! I tried to find the clearest water, but Anne wasn't much help — she started dropping stones and some sand into her bucketful — and it finally got so heavy I had to carry both. To her, water in a bucket was to be played with and we had the hardest time trying to get her to understand that this was our drinking water and hence very precious when camping out.

Back at our camp I built a couple of little fireplaces with big stones, started two fires, and put the horrible-looking water on to boil. I began gathering food and cooking utensils together and quickly discovered that we would have a major "sand" problem — every time anyone (especially Anne) walked within ten feet of the cooking area, my "kitchen" became covered with a layer of sand. One of the joys of picnicking on any beach!

Since this camping out was a spur-of-the-moment affair, we were going to have to use emergency rations for supper but we did need something for breakfast, so Merrill, J.P., and Mike decided to take off in the bush plane and head for the closest settlement. To the list of eggs, butter, etc., we added beer, ice, and ice water (by now we were hot and thirsty — our only water still tepid and muddy). So the three men took off, promising not to forget us, and we wandered along the beach, just enjoying the magnificent scenery. We couldn't imagine a more beautiful spot to be stranded in — the wide river, surrounded by virgin pine forests, green hills enclosing us, and above them, in all directions, the snow-covered mountains, the cloudless blue sky, and the hot sun. We were thinking, "What a paradise," when Lowell yelled, "There's a bear!" My first thought was: "Oh dear, he didn't SPELL the word!" Then I wondered if the animal was coming down to share the beach with us. But he was a good half mile away and seemed to be content with his particular spot. We watched him rear up on his hind legs several times, sniffing the air — he was a big one! Anne's reaction was most surprising. Before leaving home, those well-meaning people had given her the impression that Alaska was full of bears and moose — to such a point that she was quite frightened about the whole thing; that's why all the spelling. But when it came right down to seeing "the big, brown furry thing," she was fascinated. She said, "Come on, quick; let's go see him," and started dashing down the beach. We virtually had to drag her back to camp.

The little yellow plane reappeared just then and the men reported having seen many moose and bears. The only settlement they found nearby, however, was a prospector's camp, and the old man dug into his personal stores in order to provide us with eggs and butter. No beer or ice, but they did bring us a most welcome jog of cold, clear water. We felt we were cheating when we drank it, leaving the muddy river water for cooking.

Supper was fun, but hectic, cooking for four hungry men and an even hungrier child. Rice and baked beans were the sum and substance of it — our emergency rations — but delicious, and we had heaping helpfuls of the rice. Anne also had a glass of instant chocolate milk and then began the big job of trying to get her to bed. It took me from 7 P.M. until eleven, when darkness finally descended. She just would not settle down. Half the trouble was our fault: we wanted her to get into the sleeping bag, on top of an air mattress, and she would have none of it. She insisted on curling up on the canvas tent floor, preferring the wide open spaces, and we should have realized sooner that a little one doesn't need all the soft padding we old folks demand. Also she was plenty warm enough, just in her heavy wool pajamas. When we finally gave in, she slept the rest of the night on the hard tent floor, not stirring until long after we had gotten up and had breakfast the next morning.

The morning dawned a little less serenely. A strong wind was blowing when we got up at seven, and dark clouds hid the peaks to the east of us. I cooked fried eggs and coffee for everyone, amid thick-blowing sand that made everything taste decidedly granular. The tents began to flap loudly and the wind howled, but Anne slept through it all. When she finally did wake up, we were having such a sandstorm on our little peninsula that the eggs I was cooking for her became coated with sand. Poor thing — the only time on the trip so far that I really felt sorry for her. But she didn't seem a bit interested anyway, probably still sleepy, and just then one of our tents blew down, creating general pandemonium all about her. I did manage to get a cup of chocolate milk down her and I figured that would keep her going until we reached some kind of civilization.

Once the tent collapsed, we made great haste to pack up all the gear and get off that sand bar. Back on the grass it was wonderful to be out of the blowing sand. We were thoroughly coated with it — teeth and all — and it was days before we finally got the last of it out of all our belongings.

The flight that day was, needless to say, one of the roughest yet, thanks to the strong wind. But at least the weather was clear, as usual. (We felt extremely fortunate to have been blessed with blue sky for every flight all the way from home.) The terrain was mostly virgin pine forests to Watson Lake (we crossed into the Yukon there), where we refueled at the usual RCAF outpost. It was noon by now, and the three men in Merrill's plane refused to budge another step without some food under their belts. As chief cook, I felt a little guilty — our sand-bar meals must have been a bit on the meager side. But Lowell and I couldn't face the half-hour ride to town and back and decided to cook some dehydrated soup on our primus stove in a hangar. That turned out to be a great success — Anne had several helpings of delicious hot vegetable soup, a glass of chocolate milk, and three lollipops. Quite contented, she crawled back into her seat and was asleep the minute we took off.

The rest of the flight to Whitehorse was a series of the bumpiest bumps I had ever experienced, over the most rugged terrain imaginable. The land beneath us was a jumbled mass of rock-strewn hills, narrow, forested valleys, and deep river gorges. Snow-covered mountains rose above this ragged landscape in all directions, as far as we could see — the wilderness of the Yukon that we had always heard so much about.

> "There's the land. (Have you seen it?)
> It's the cussedest land I know,
>   from the big, dizzy mountains that screen it
> To the deep, death-like valleys below.
>   Some say God was tired when he made it;
>   Some say it's a fine land to shun;
>   Maybe: but there's some as would trade it
>   For no land on earth — and I'm one."
>   (ROBERT W. SERVICE)

This was the land of Sam McGee, Dangerous Dan McGrew, One-eyed Mike, and the "lady known as Lou." It's really questionable as to who gave the Yukon its greatest renown, Robert W. Service or the Klondike gold rush. Service spent three years as a teller in a bank at Whitehorse, and his poems immortalize the inhabitants, the beauty, and the romance of this region. We would have loved to stay in Whitehorse and visit Sam McGee's cabin or try to find out more about the "lady known as Lou," but we could only land at the airport long enough to check with Customs and re-fuel the plane.

We did fly low over some of the old river boats tied up at the docks — Whitehorse is at the head of Yukon River navigation and when gold was discovered in the Klondike, these river boats and many others carried thousands of people north to Dawson and the Klondike area. Northwest Mounted Police records show that over 7000 boats, with 28,000 people, passed Whitehorse in 1898 (and only 3500 live there today!). The Yukon narrow-gauge railroad (built a few years later) ran from Whitehorse south to Skagway, on the coast, where the hordes of gold seekers first reached Alaska by boat. But until it was built, these men and women had to walk the entire route.

Now we followed this railroad and trail down toward the coast, first through a wide flat valley, then into one of the most famous of American landmarks, the White Pass. Tremendous mountains of rock, snow, and glaciers rose above us, the steep rock canyon walls descending to a jumbled mass of rock, ice, and water below — Dead Horse Gulch, a place of terror to thousands of gold-rush seekers who followed this "trail of '98." Parts of the trail could still be seen among the canyons and boulders. We wondered how those poor people and animals ever made it in mid-winter — how strong the lure of gold! And how easily we slipped between those mountains that day, the snow and ice glittering in the sun and deep blue sky everywhere above us. How easy with the engine running, but if it had ever quit, where could we have landed? Lowell and I both worried about it during our entire transit of the pass — he looked over all those snow-covered slopes, thinking perhaps we could set down there. I looked at all the little semi-frozen lakes, thinking that perhaps the ice might be strong enough to hold us. Horrible thoughts, which made the pass a place of terror for us in a way, too. Then, just beyond a rocky slope up ahead, we spotted the blue water of the Pacific. Balboa couldn't have been any happier than we! We had about a half hour's flight left, just due south, down the Lynn Canal, those mountains still all about us. Then around a rocky, tree-covered point and down to the Juneau airport. What a day it had been!

Incidentally, I didn't have to wake Anne this time when

we were about to land. She had been awake during the whole last flight, not watching the magnificent scenery — oh no — the entire time she had her nose buried in a comic book!

CHAPTER III

A Guy Named Joe

Juneau, Alaska's capital, has a population of
7500 and is built up against Mount Juneau, with the Gastineau Channel at its foot. The hills around the town are
thickly covered with green pine, and snow-covered mountains
are everywhere. (The snow melted from the lower mountains during the month we were there.) The town and its
setting reminded both of us of Darjeeling, India. It has a
slightly run-down look, not modern and shiny. Most of the
buildings and homes are wooden and weather-beaten, in need
of a new coat of paint. There are few big pretentious houses,
even the governor's mansion, although an imposing white co-
lonial home, has a small back yard, and is almost hidden among
other less fancy buildings. Of course, construction costs are
terrifyingly high there — in fact, everything is expensive because it all has to come in by ship or plane. And then the
people are the unpretentious kind — friendly and easygoing.
No one seems to be thinking of impressing anyone else, no
one (but us) appears to be in a hurry. There are no traffic

lights, cars stop for other cars, and always for pedestrians, the drivers smiling genially and giving you plenty of time to get across. The people usually smile at you on the sidewalks, and storekeepers treat you like their best friend. Anyone can charge anything, it is said, and very few have ever cheated. The one or two who did were caught at the airport on the way out. The one local highway becomes a dead end just thirty miles beyond town, so one could not escape very far in a car. (A branch of the Alaska Highway comes as far south as Haines, which is near Skagway, at the head of the Lynn Canal. In the summertime a ferry makes several round trips a week between Haines and Juneau.)

The streets in town are narrow and winding, and the stores have a frontierlike appearance. It's impossible to get lost there — you can see the modern six-story Baranof hotel from all over town, and there is only one main street, a steep one running straight up the hill. In fact, one is always climbing up or down, and the roads on different levels are connected by steep wooden stairways. (When standing on a hilltop, looking down toward the water, you can see the roads doubling back and forth, each a little lower down the hillside, those steep stairways joining them all together.)

A towering rock face provides a dramatic backdrop for the northwest part of town, and a lovely thin waterfall cascades down its full length. At the bottom it becomes Gold Nugget Creek, the stream where a guy named Joe Juneau first discovered gold in the area and set up his camp. Now the town has grown up around this little mountain stream and it is treated like a shrine, completely fenced in all the way down to the cannel, with concrete sides and bottom.

Joe Juneau and a fellow prospector, Dick Harris, made their discovery in 1880, but their camp wasn't overrun by a wild stampede such as happened in the Klondike or at Nome.

Some gold seekers did come up from Sitka (then the capital of Alaska), and Juneau (first called Harrisburg, Pilzburg, and Rockwell) became the first Alaskan white settlement founded under the American flag. The capital was moved there in 1900.

The most extraordinary things were always happening when we were there, helping to remind us that we weren't just in a small midwestern town. Several days after we first arrived a young thirty-foot humpback whale was chased up on a beach near the airport by a pack of killer whales, and no one talked about anything else for two days. All were concerned for the poor whale's welfare — the tide had gone out, leaving him stranded, and he would die if he dried out. So neighborhood children started a bucket brigade, keeping him "watered" with their little beach pails. Then the fire department took over, spraying him with its hoses. Finally some neighbors (I wonder whether they were concerned over the whale's safety or the overwhelming stench that could be the final result) rounded up boats and tried towing him out to sea. They tried three times, and he always returned to the beach again. On the fourth attempt he turned over and was drowned. Juneau practically went into mourning.

The next day an Alaskan National Guard C–47 landed at the airport. Several officials walked out to greet it (some army brass coming, we thought), the door opened, and out wobbled seventeen baby moose! They were so little that they ran up and snuggled against us, sucking our fingers and whimpering like puppy dogs. They had been captured by helicopter when they were just a few days old, and now they were being transported to a wooded area just south of Juneau which the Wildlife Service wanted populated with moose.

They were so cute that we decided to follow them out

to their temporary pens in order to take some pictures. What an undertaking that became — children and animals may be difficult to photograph but baby moose are impossible, especially seventeen of them in one enclosure. When J.P. and Mike entered the pen, the moose must have thought they were their long-lost parents. They swarmed around the two men, nuzzling them, sucking their hands and fingers, chewing on their shirts. It was comical, but the two men were most embarrassed by so much affection. The moose went after the camera and tripod, too, licking the wood, chewing on the rubber-tipped handle. One even licked the lens. This made picture-taking difficult, to say the least; every time Mike got ready to shoot, a moose would snuggle up against him, lick his face, or nudge the camera.

Mike and J.P. quickly decided that they couldn't work with seventeen moose milling around, so they herded most of them into a little corral, leaving four in the big pen. Then the two men walked toward the back of the pen to find a good background location. Once they were set up, Anne and I joined them, and Anne had a field day, kissing, hugging, and patting the moose to her heart's content and being licked all over in return. But we had a time getting a picture of one with Anne. The men took turns luring them on, letting them suck fingers until they got to Anne, but instead of staying with her, they wandered right on after the men — they seemed far more interested in grownups than in children. One frisky one came toward Anne, who was sitting on the ground, and then suddenly turned around and kicked out at her with his hind legs. His hoofs hit her right on the chest. I heard the loud thump and froze with fright. Then Anne started to whimper and we all rushed toward her. Apparently he had caught her at the end of his kick, so it was a light blow, and she was only upset that her furry friend should kick instead of lick. J.P. picked the moose right up in his arms and carried him, bawling, back to the corral.

That ended the moose photography as far as I was concerned. From now on, I would avoid tame little baby animals. We did stay long enough to watch them being fed, however. The attendants combined Carnation milk with water and Pablum, then poured the mixture into special buckets, with two rubber "teats" sticking out from the bottoms, and the little ones gobbled up their supper. The next day they would be back in the woods again, having to forage for themselves. (The Wildlife people planned to keep them in captivity for as short a time as possible, so that the animals would not forget how to find food on their own.)

The following morning, Juneau greeted us with another rip-roaring surprise. Anne and I had just gone up to our hotel room after breakfast when suddenly the whole building seemed to shake with an ear-splitting explosion. I was wondering whether a boiler had blown up or a guest had decided to do away with himself, when Lowell burst into the room with the explanation — he had been standing in the lobby watching a group of hunters leave the elevator, .375 Magnum rifles slung over their shoulders. They were talking about the Alaskan brown bears that they would shoot that day when one of the monstrous guns suddenly went off. After the smoke cleared, they were all looking up at a two-inch hole in the ceiling, undoubtedly thankful that no one in the crowded lobby had been hit. The manager was wiping his brow with relief, when he suddenly realized that the bullet must have gone into the floor above. That couple still in Room 210 just overhead — he raced upstairs and knocked on their door. It was opened by an irate man clad in a bath towel, holding his *derriére*. "Who the heck was hammering on my bathtub!" Come to Alaska and live dangerously, even in the state's most luxurious Baranof Hotel!

We began thinking that Alaskan brown bears must be awfully big if one had to use gunpowder like that to stop them, and then we met the man who confirmed our suspicions. Rod Darnell, a well-known hunter and fisherman in Juneau, told us that this particular type of bear, so prevalent in the area, is the largest carnivorous animal in the world. Some, when they stand up, are nearly ten feet tall and weigh close to a ton. One day a few years ago Rod went hunting with two men on nearby Chichagof Island. He had gone ahead of his friends and had rounded some bushes when he suddenly found himself facing three huge bears. Two were yearlings weighing only five or six hundred pounds. The mother was more than twice that size, almost as big as an elephant. The two little ones ran away, but the mother charged in an instant. Darnell just barely had time to raise his gun and fire, hitting the bear in the head. The bear kept coming, and Darnell knew that the maddened animal would now try to break his neck with one swipe of her huge paw. So he whirled around and threw himself down on the ground, clasping his hands behind his head. His friends appeared just then, saw the bear flinging Darnell about, tearing him apart, the man's head in the animal's huge jaws. One of the men was finally able to shoot the bear dead, and they found Darnell still conscious. His arm, chest, and shoulder were terribly torn, and his scalp was ripped loose. They doubted that he would ever make the seventy miles back to Juneau in their small boat. There was a salmon cannery fairly nearby, so they took him there, then sent a short-wave message to Juneau. A doctor flew down in a Grumman Goose and flew him back to the Juneau hospital. Today he has some ugly scars, but most people think it miraculous that he has lived to tell the story. And he still guides and hunts!

We did hear one amusing bear story, if that's possible. A construction worker left his truck-door open one day while working in a fairly remote area. One of those huge brown bears climbed in, smelling the picnic lunch. The man returned to find the bear sitting in the cab, munching away. Before he thought, he slammed the door, imprisoning the bear within the cab, and then had to face a truck repair bill of $700! I never did find out who finally let the bear out, and how.

Charlie over the Fairweather Range

Camping on a Liard River sand bar

Anne, Tay, and Merrill Wien on the Juneau Icecap

Daddy's beard is pretty rough

Anne and Tay at Camp 10

The Thomas family on the Juneau Icecap

Anne hitches a ride on the ice field

Sawyer Glacier

CHAPTER IV

The Movie Stars Quit
and Turn Tourist

W<small>E</small> all thought Juneau was a most fascinating, charming town, but before we could really explore it, Anne and I had to do our bit of work in return for the privilege of coming on the trip. Our first job, once we got there, was to finish filming our camping sequence — the family, on the way to Alaska, landing on the highway to spend the night. The shenanigans we went through to get this one simple five-minute scene! I had never known what was involved in professional movie work before this and I'm glad I didn't. First, the men had to spend two days looking for the right setting. They finally located a small air strip a half hour away by air (near Haines), a stream of sorts beside it, and snow-covered mountains for a backdrop. They set up the tent by the only patch of green bushes, hiding some tin cans and a few old rusted plane parts in the process. The "stream" was a filthy stagnant pool of water and in

order to make it look like running water on film we all
took turns throwing rocks into it. Then another two days of
equipment troubles (they used two 35 mm. movie cameras
on heavy tripods, a generator to run the cameras and sound
equipment, two tape recorders, lights, reflectors, camera
slates, and so forth), endless delays, it seemed to me, and
a frightful waste of unusually sunny weather. Lowell and I
were used to "shooting from the hip" with a small 16 mm.
camera only.

Finally J.P. and Mike were ready for us, and we spent two
long days (and many more hours after that) commuting back
and forth, working there from nine in the morning until
six at night. Anne didn't seem to mind the odd goings on a
bit. She slept in the plane and played all over the airfield,
clambering over several airplane wrecks, throwing stones
into that running water, and filling one of the cooking pots
with everything from wild flowers and clover to the director's chalk. Several times J.P. and Mike stopped what they
were doing in order to follow her with the camera. At one
time the lens was no more than a foot from her face, but
she was so intent on what she was doing that she paid no
attention whatsoever.

One of the scenes we worked on was a brief one of Anne
and me leaving the airplane to join Lowell by the tent. With
the camera rolling, I jumped out, turned to Anne in the
back seat, said, "Come on, let's get out and join Daddy —— "
"NO," said she, curling up with thumb in mouth. "Cut,"
yelled J.P. Daddy yelled more than that. With a threatened
strike on our hands, we decided to skip that scene for the
moment. It was late in the day by now and our "star" was
feeling rather sleepy. We went on to others: Lowell putting
up the tent, me getting water in that miserable stream and,
with Anne's help, washing clothes in the water. It wasn't

difficult to persuade her to perform this chore, and both J.P. and Mike sacrificed dry socks to the cause. Mike went right out into the water with the camera and tripod to get a closer shot of Anne, and J.P. set the microphone on a stand out in the water, too, hoping to catch some of her mumbled jargon. In the middle of the scene the mike fell over — gurgle, gurgle, gurgle. More delay.

It was getting late the next day when we came to our final scene — a peaceful one of the family sitting in front of the tent eating supper. J.P. suggested I put Anne in her pajamas to make it more homey — howls of protest. "O.K., O.K., just say it's time to go to bed and take her into the tent." Hmmmmm, this might look very similar to bedtime scenes at home. Anyway, we decided to give it a try. I had opened a can of meatballs, to be realistic, and made a pass at heating them over the primus stove. "O.K., rolling," said J.P. "Speed," said Mike. "Scene 73, take one," read the inevitable camera slate. A nod from J.P. and I asked Lowell if he wanted another helping of meat. He made a mere gesture of eating one bite, then said, "No more, thank you," and I turned to Anne. She was supposed to decline, too, and then I was to bring up the subject of bed. Obviously she had not read the script. "I'd love some more," she said and promptly proceeded to eat the entire can of cold greasy meatballs. So there we sat, in absolute silence, the camera grinding away. I couldn't say, "All right, bed," right in the middle of a mouthful of meat. We finally did get to the bedtime scene, and it was a typical one. We had to repeat it three or four times in order to get close-ups of all of us. Each time one of us said, "All right, Anne, bedtime," even if she was way over on the other side of the air strip at that moment, she would recoil with alarm and yell, "No, I won't." But we did get what we wanted and really went home to bed.

All this shooting of one sequence scattered over so many days created a big "wardrobe" problem that had never occurred to me at home. We had to wear exactly the same clothing each day that we went to the air strip, so that when all the camping film was eventually put together it would appear as one uninterrupted scene. As a result, we began looking like bums. Anne got so dirty that I had to wash the same sweater, pants, and shirt every evening, drying them over radiators or on *Charlie*'s tail in the sun the next morning. I should have brought along duplicates of everything.

Our last day of work in Juneau was spent in *Charlie*, just circling about the Juneau area, getting pictures of us in flight. J.P. and Mike took hours to rig up batteries in the back seat, plus lights, large camera, and tape recorder. Then they squeezed in, too. It was a struggle to close the doors, and, once in, they could barely move more than the camera button. We climbed in front, Anne on my lap (she was not supposed to be in these pictures but there was no one to leave her with on the ground), and *Charlie* took off easily, despite the full load. Anne went to sleep right away, so she was no problem, but we certainly had plenty of others! Not problems really— just so much to do; flying the plane, watching for other traffic, remembering what we were supposed to say, and then trying to act it out in front of the camera. I was supposed to look tired and concerned, anxious to land for the night. I "hammed" my way through several takes — I just could not feel that way. Finally Lowell took the plane over to a small mountain and started zooming along at treetop level, following the slopes up and then diving back down again. I started yelling and shouting, pleading, most upset and worried. All the time the camera was grinding away in the back seat. I was also getting madder and madder at Lowell and his cohorts for playing such a mean trick. When

J.P. finally yelled, "Cut," I was fit to be tied. Lowell went up to a more sensible altitude; J.P. said, "That was a nice piece of acting, Tay," and I was ready to shove them all out *Charlie*'s door!

Later Mike moved to the co-pilot's seat with the camera, (J.P. was left at the airport) while I held the lights, sitting in one corner of Anne's back seat, and we took pictures of her there, doing what she usually does on a flight: lying down and sucking her thumb, looking out the window while sucking her thumb, and reading while sucking her thumb — that will look familiar to a lot of parents!

It was good to have our part in the film work finished, and the first excursion Anne and I made together, while the men were still working on aerial photography, was to visit the Mendenhall Glacier, the only one in Alaska directly reached by highway. We borrowed Lowell's rented car, drove thirteen miles out along the Glacier Highway, following signs, and were amazed by what we found: a great jagged wall of ice almost two miles wide, with only a few hundred yards of water between it and the gravel bar we were standing on. Covered with deep cracks and holes, the glacier has a lovely blue tinge of color, which becomes a deep blue down in the bigger cracks. The water in front of it is dotted with large chunks of ice that have broken off — "little iceboooorgs," Anne called them. We actually saw one fall off on one of our later visits, the piece, the size of a small car making a loud roar and a terrific splash as it hit the water. Even a little one can make big waves which come way up on the gravel bar, so I can understand now why great walls of cascading ice from a moving glacier make such a tremendous spectacle.

The area in front of the glacier is a national park, and yet we seldom saw other people there. It was a perfect spot for a quiet retreat, and we went a number of times in the follow-

ing weeks, often taking picnics along. Little paths wandered
in and out among the cliffs and boulders, and Anne spent
hours following them. I found an inscription on one rock
which read "Glacier level *here* — 1938," almost two miles
from the present glacier "foot." It is retreating fast, leaving
a wide moraine and remnants of a buried forest behind.
When Juneau wanted to build a big new airport recently,
the only available land large and level enough was on the
wide Mendenhall moraine.

Another favorite pastime for us in Juneau was swimming,
thereby proving Alaska isn't just a land of snow and ice!
The weather man smiled upon us during most of our month
in town. Juneau ordinarily has mild winters (milder than ours
in New Jersey) and cool rainy summers. The average temperature then is sixty-five degrees. When the sun is out it
can be much warmer, and summer clothes are a must. When
it is cloudy, and the winds blow in from the sea, the temperatures drop into the fifties, and we had to return to our
sweaters and coats. We were blessed with two solid weeks
of cloudless skies and eighty-degree temperatures.

One such day, when we all had a little time off, we drove
west of town to look for a public beach. We did find
one and had a good swim, but instead of sand there were
countless sharp, barnacle-covered rocks — rugged on the feet.
But then you don't go to Alaska for its beaches. I noticed
that all the local children wore bathing shoes or sneakers, so
they weren't a bit bothered. The water was surprisingly warm,
like Long Island Sound in late June, yet we paddled about
with the snow-covered mountains all around us. (The warm
Japanese current explains this phenomenon.)

We explored a bit and discovered another public bathing
spot, a lovely small lake near the glacier. The water was
clear and warm, due to some hot springs, and there was

coarse brown sand around the edges. Anne had great fun here, especially because she could paddle about with other little children just her age. This, I felt, was one of my most important "duties" on arriving in Juneau — to seek out play-mates for Anne. It was hard at first. We saw them passing by on the streets or playing in their yards, but we could just look on. Then we discovered the lake, and I asked one of the mothers there one day if there was a playground in town. She told me about "Evergreen Bowl," so off we started on another exploration trip. We found it about a mile away from the hotel, a small pine tree-bordered park beside Gold Nugget Creek, with a baseball diamond, two tennis courts, two swimming pools, and plenty of swings and seesaws. The place swarmed with children of all ages, and Anne had no trouble "picking up" several friends every time we went. I usually sat by the creek under a pine tree, reading, while Anne cavorted all over the area — what a wonderful chance for her to blow off steam! In fact, she was usually so tired by the time we headed for home that the long walk back was torture for us both. It took a long time anyway; we always had to look in all the store windows, going and coming, we had to "tightrope walk" all the wide curbs or stone walls, then climb up and down a big green railing, walk backward up some of the steps, sit on others to rest, and stop and watch any child or adult we passed. It was the same ritual every time, and it certainly gave me a good chance to observe the goings on around us.

First I concentrated on the people and reaffirmed what we felt earlier, that everyone was pleasant and friendly. They all smiled, many would comment on the weather, and every-body would talk to Anne or help her up a step or off a curb. And another thing I noticed — when the weather was sunny, but in the sixties (typical Juneau summer weather), Anne and I wore sweaters, skirts, and light coats, as we would at home. But Alaskan women were wearing summer cottons, with no sweaters at all. They are either more used to the cold or else, because they have a shorter summer season, they feel they must start dressing for it in May. They also seem much more used to the rainy weather, going outside as usual, often even without raincoats. The children swim every day during the summer, regardless of pouring rain or freezing cold. A rugged people!

The stores there are the same one would find in any of the smaller towns back home — the same clothes, food, and toys, but less variety, and the prices gave us a shock. Everything is at least thirty per cent higher. One cucumber costs forty-nine cents, one can of soup is twenty-three cents, a pound of tomatoes is fifty-five cents, carrots or celery are twenty-seven cents a pound, milk is sixty cents a quart, a good bottle of scotch costs ten dollars, and a short beer is seventy cents! The one store window that always amused me was the local flower shop — it was bare except for two fake poppy wreaths and one droopy philodendron plant. Edna Ferber was right when she mentioned in *Ice Palace* that roses and orchids were rare there!

Just beyond the store area, we always passed one of the public schools. I had been hearing from all sides that students in Alaskan public schools maintain higher grades and have higher intelligence quotients than those of pupils in the rest of the states. Fewer Alaskan children drop out before finishing high school, and, according to one national magazine survey, Alaskans over sixteen years of age have a general educational level two years higher than the average for all other states. Dr. William Keller, head of the education department at the University of Alaska, explains that it is because of their climate: school activity is concentrated indoors.

Also, Alaska's school system is conservatively run — they stick mainly to the three R's and don't go in for the frills that have become the fashion in the other states. And (kids take note!) students in Alaskan schools get more homework to do, too.

We had also heard that every Alaskan community — Eskimo, Indian, or white — has its own grade school, and only five per cent of the students live in areas where there are no high schools.

The most glamorous building we passed on our walks was the three-storied gleaming white governor's mansion sitting on top of a hill. The view from the many columned porch must be glorious — of the town below, the deep blue Gastineau Channel, and the mountains beyond. The ten bedrooms inside were a great help to the then Governor Mike Stepovich because he and his wife had eight children, ranging from nine years down to one. "All the little Steps," they are often called. They were away in California at that time, or I am sure we would have seen hordes of children running about the mansion's lawn, chasing around the official flagpole, or climbing up the magnificent two-story totem pole leaning against the side of the house. We saw totem poles of all sizes and colors — many were imitations of the old, painted in garish colors to catch the eye of the tourist, but my favorite was the governor's because most of its wood was stained a deep mahogany, while dark greens and reds highlighted the grotesque faces. The Juneau area is the home of the totem pole, thanks to the Haida and Tlingit Indians who have been making them for hundreds of years. Since before recorded history, the Tlingits were the seafarers and fishermen of southeastern Alaska. They lived in good comfort in large, well-constructed villages, in a mild and healthy climate. Their forests and waters abounded with game and fish. The first white settlers found them to be thrifty and intelligent, and hard workers, especially when it came to carving totem poles! They started cutting huge cedar logs into faces of people and animals for three different occasions: for ritualistic ceremonies when the figures told the story of legends or past events, to honor their dead (with the crest of the family of the dead person carved on top), or to shame their enemies. This one was erected by a rival chief before the house of another chief who had broken his word or had done something equally dishonorable. These poles were rare, as the mere threat was usually enough.

Today the Tlingits number only about 8000 (there are two other smaller Indian tribes who total about 7000), and gone are their community houses, ceremonials, war canoes, and totem-pole carving. Now they dress and live much the same as their fellow white citizens. But they have left an indelible imprint on Alaska through the totem poles and the many geographical names derived from the Tlingit language, such as Sitka, Taku, Tongass, Yakutat, and Ketchikan. They also have the more dubious distinction of contributing the word "hootch" to our vocabulary! It comes from the Indian word "hoochinoo," which was a potent drink they made from molasses.

I had gone to Alaska believing that all the native peoples there were Eskimos. I quickly found out how wrong I was. Besides the Indians, I also learned about the Aleuts, a branch of the Eskimo family who live in the Aleutian Islands. The Aleuts take the prize in the contribution of geographical names: the word Alaska comes from the Aleut "A-la-as-ka" meaning "the great country." They live in the Aleutian Islands, along the Alaska Peninsula, and on Kodiak Island. Many of them live in the Pribilofs where they work in the government fur-sealing operations.

Their language is similar to Eskimo, and every island has

its own variation. But they also have amalgamated with their white neighbors, rather than preserving old customs, and there are only about 4000 of them left. In a way, we were sorry that they had lost their past because they had some of the most unusual and colorful customs. Their earliest homes were built underground for protection against the stormy climate. Now they use wooden shacks. Instead of the now prevalent khaki pants and T shirts, the men used to wear long skirts of feathered birdskins and the women dressed in fur sealskins. They made raincoats from seal intestines. We found it very hard to believe, but we were told that some of them went barefooted all year round.

Besides the playground, our other favorite haunt in Juneau was the waterfront. Lowell took us down to see the fishing fleet one day, hundreds of colorful little cabin cruisers tied to the many long wharves. Anne was fascinated with the huge nets spread out to dry, the horrible fishy smell, and the weather-beaten men who usually live aboard, often with their families, too. The salmon season hadn't started yet, but the boats went out each day for halibut. Almost everybody owns a boat for pleasure — going fishing on weekends, often catching five or six salmon and trout at a time. Many of the cab drivers drive cabs during the winter, then fish commercially for halibut and salmon for five months during the warm season.

The waterfront is a busy place, but Anne's favorite section was the seaplane base, and we spent hours on a dock opposite it, watching the planes being loaded and taxiing in and out. This was the Alaska Coastal Airlines' busy terminal. They have about nineteen amphibious planes, providing scheduled service throughout southeastern Alaska. There were always planes taking off or landing. Often the co-pilot would crawl out on a wing while they taxied in or out, due to tough wind conditions probably. The planes tied up at floats at least thirty to fifty feet below the hangars on the docks because of the fifty-foot tide. Then if any maintenance was required, the planes were hoisted up on giant elevators.

Obviously we didn't have to spend much time in our hotel room, which was good as far as a two-year-old is concerned. The Baranof is the latest word in modern luxury, and our two rooms were large, with magnificent views of the town and harbor. So we had every comfort that a home could provide. In fact, one day when Anne was following her friend, the hotel maid, from room to room, she pointed to her own and said, "That's my home." How quickly they adjust!

Hotel meals were a problem, however, the dining room not opening early enough for little children. That's when our electric cooker became so useful. Anne feasted on cucumbers, carrots, canned vegetables, soups, and rice. An informal cafeteria was open for breakfast, and we all ate there together. Anne loved eating with the men, especially Merrill. Yes, our daughter had fallen madly in love with an Alaskan bush pilot. She acted just like a lovesick teen-ager, keeping everyone amused but Mummie and Daddy, who were beginning to wonder what she'd be like twelve years from now if she was so badly off now. She finally paid him the highest compliment of all by changing the name of her favorite moth-eaten grubby rabbit from "Fooey" to Merrill.

Anne's other great friend was the "alligator man" (elevator, in our language), who was an Indian. She assumed he was an Eskimo and asked where his fur parka was. A typical tourist!

Our biggest problem in traveling with a child in Alaska was that infernal midnight sun. It was a joy to have many more daylight hours for work and play out of doors (the men often worked with their cameras until 8 or 9 P.M.), but when it came to putting Anne to bed at night, it was a real curse. Juneau was still as bright as midday at six o'clock at night, and there was twilight until almost eleven o'clock. Then it became light again by four in the morning. I went through an elaborate ritual each night, trying to darken Anne's room: I hung a blanket, one bedspread, and three or four towels up over each window in a desperate attempt to block out the daz-zling sun. A lot of good it did! I was lucky if she went to sleep by nine-thirty. And I knew the problem would become much worse as we went farther north. Many of the women who live in Alaska told me that their children quickly became used to the sunlit nights, but those who did have trouble often covered bedroom windows with aluminum foil.

Before we left home, friends warned me that I'd feel aw-fully tied down by a two-year-old in the evenings, but it wasn't nearly as tough as I had expected. I ate early dinner with Anne, while Lowell usually joined the men. (It gave them a good chance to get away from "us women.") And I dis-covered that the evenings were the only time that I had for reading or writing. Occasionally J.P. and Mike volunteered to be baby sitters, much to Anne's delight, and while they played chess, we went out to see the town. The most famous night spot in Juneau was the Red Dog Saloon — we pushed through the swinging doors, sat at tables decked with red-checked tablecloths, and danced on the sawdust-covered floors to the ragtime piano tunes of Hattie Jessup. Hattie, who was over seventy but looked years younger, had played piano backgrounds for many of the silent movies, and how she could still make those keys talk!

How easy it was to think we were back in the Gold Rush era: the waiter with his beard and handlebar mustache, the stuffed animal heads on the wall, the dancing-girl pictures,

the old-time guns, and the Confederate flag all helped create
the atmosphere of those wild early days. And to make the
evening complete we were served drinks filled with ice straight
from the Mendenhall Glacier!

CHAPTER V

Runaway Glaciers and a

Sea of Ice

THE time had come for the Juneau Icecap expedition, and Lowell Thomas, Sr., and some of his expert skier friends came out to join Lowell. Maynard Miller and a group of Juneau Icefield Research Program scientists also flew in. Maynard is an old friend of both Thomases — a superdynamic, superenergetic young man with an equally superwinning personality. He is a glaciologist who has specialized in this particular area.

The icecap, a huge sea of almost unbroken ice, lies in a mountain basin just behind Mount Juneau, an isolated wilderness for men traveling on foot, but by plane it can be reached in twenty minutes. Merrill's plane was equipped with skis, so along with a local pilot, Ken Loken, he flew in the entire party, making many trips, including a number of freight hauls. When at the other end, he merely opened the plane door and pushed the baggage out.

Anne and I would have to stay behind in Juneau for two weeks, and, to make the trying period even more difficult, the weather turned bad, raining almost continuously. But that was when we met the Stewarts — great good luck for us! Tom Stewart is a young lawyer in Juneau. He was born and grew up there (his father was mayor for many years), went to Yale Law School, and came back home to hang out his shingle just a few years ago. (In November 1958 he was elected to the State Senate.) He's a great skier and a friend of Maynard Miller's. (Somehow Maynard found time amid the mad rush of expedition preparation to introduce me to them.) He and his wife, Jane, have five children, eleven, nine, seven, five, and a six-month-old baby girl, and live in a large, old rambling house about six blocks from the hotel. They welcomed us into their home and we spent every day there, all the children vying for Anne's attention. They played together in the attic or the cellar or, when the weather finally got better, out on their lawn where there were swings, slide, and a plastic pool and hose.

I spent my days in their homey family kitchen, working over my typewriter or taking care of the baby while Jane gave piano lessons (she is a very talented musician). In fact, the whole house fairly bursts with music. The three older children each play the piano and another instrument, so the three pianos in the house are going from early morning until bedtime. I also had a good chance to learn a little about living in Alaska through them. Of course, life there is very much as it is in almost any small town anywhere in America, except for the extraordinarily high cost of living. But the people there also seem more "worldly" — they travel a lot — seem most interested in foreign affairs, and many of the young people go all the way to the East Coast for their education. It seems the custom to send even the littlest children "out" (to the other states) for their vacations or summer holidays.

And their life is not only more easygoing and unpretentious but also very much of an outdoor one. Because Juneau is a small town, the children walk to school, walk to church, walk to the playground. The winters are relatively mild so they are out of doors almost as much as in the summer, everyone ice skating or skiing (Douglas, the town just across the channel, has a small rope-tow ski development. Some of the more expert skiers fly up to the Icecap in the springtime). Many of the mountains behind the town have trails, novice or difficult, for those who like to hike and climb. The Stewarts took four of their children on an all-day hike out near the glacier shortly before we arrived. And, of course, hunting and fishing play a big part in the lives of many of the people here. The forests are teeming with bear, moose, and deer, and the salmon and trout are abundant in the channel. Many families have small boats, and some have cabins on isolated islands which they visit over weekends in the summertime. (The Stewarts take all of their children on such excursions.) Other Juneau families own one-room cabins along the beaches outside of town and spend their summer weekends there. We had half a dozen invitations from friends to visit them for a picnic or a swim at their "retreat."

Whenever there was a break in the weather, Anne and I drove out to the Mendenhall Glacier. I sat on a rock and looked up at that immense river of ice, wondering what the men were up to at the other end and how everything was going. Ocassionally, on clear days, we would spot Merrill's little yellow plane flying above the Mendenhall, on his way to or from the expedition with supplies and messages. Fifteen other glaciers come down from that almost 1500 square miles of unbroken, blindingly white ice field. It is 4–7000 feet high, a miniature Greenland plateau. And it is only a small part of the world's largest glaciated area there in southeastern Alaska. This area extends along the coast from the Stikine River in the south up almost to the Aleutian Islands — 2000 miles of great glaciers and spectacular fiords. And those 2000 miles also include hundreds of breathtaking mountains — some rising 17- and 18,000 feet straight from the sea. Their high slopes are the birthplace of the glaciers. The warm moist winds of the Japanese current cause the extremely heavy snowfall all along this coastal range — more falls every winter than can melt in the summer, so the surplus packs down and forms masses of ice. This has gone on for centuries, the ice being constantly pushed on toward the sea by newer snowfalls.

A group of scientists, those led by Maynard Miller, have been studying these glaciers for the last ten years. They built a small permanent camp on the then unnamed, unexplored icecap. Lowell Thomas visited them there eight years ago, and now his television series was going to include another visit to this remote little-known spot. Maynard had discovered that most of these glaciers have been retreating during the century (174 in the whole area have been studied — of these, sixty-one per cent are retreating, only 6 per cent are advancing — the rest are standing still). The Taku and Mendenhall glaciers lie almost next to each other, both receiving snow and ice from the same general source. Yet the former is advancing and the latter is retreating, a real puzzle! Maynard has found that the advancing glaciers are the longest and largest ones and contain more ice than all the others put together. The Taku is a huge frozen river of ice forty miles long and is the only glacier of the sixteen on the icecap which is advancing. Their field studies reveal that these Juneau glaciers are replenished by snow or rain from two different altitude levels. The upper level is from 5–6000 feet, and the lower one is about 3–4000 feet. Before World War I, more snow fell in the lower level, and those glaciers (fed at that altitude) advanced. Since 1920 Juneau records show that the average yearly temperature has risen eight degrees. The result? The snows at that lower level have turned to rain, the glaciers involved are retreating, and the other glaciers, fed by heavier snowfalls from the upper level, are now advancing.

Maynard and his scientists further suspect that these warming trends come in forty-year cycles and are probably related to the forty-year sunspot cycles. During periods of no sunspot activity the climate has been relatively cool and dry. We are now approaching the end of the period of high sunspot activity and warmer weather, so it looks like winters will be getting more severe! (One of their methods of checking on these cycles is extremely interesting: they bore deep into the ice with long metal tubes, and the cores they pull out are marked with rings, just like those inside trees, only vertical instead of horizontal — the "ice rings" representing the snowfall for a certain period of time. Maynard considers the glaciers gigantic weather stations which have recorded the climatic conditions for centuries — it is now merely a problem of deciphering the recorded data.)

One bleak rainy day, Anne and I got a radio message from the icecap: "Come visit us when the weather is good." Great excitement! I dug out all our ski clothes, fretted over the lack of goggles for Anne (one could go blind in a few hours on the brilliant snow at that time of year), and worried over inadequate sun hats for both of us. The biggest problem was the bad weather. When would it ever clear?

Then on Friday (the 13th) Merrill (who had been grounded in Juneau by the weather) said he thought it might break up enough the next day for our great excursion. Saturday morning dawned cloudy as usual, but we rushed out to the airport at eight in hopes of getting off. The mountains were all above the clouds, the visibility was poor, and the daily 8 A.M. weather report from the icecap said, "Zero, zero." I was so disappointed! We frittered away a couple of hours back at the hotel, and by eleven there seemed to be a slight improvement in ceiling and visibility. (There was no way of knowing what it would be like on the icecap because there would be no more radio contact until 5 P.M.) We rushed back to the airport, and Merrill decided to give it a try. I put Anne on my lap in the co-pilot's seat, and off we went.

We had good visibility all the way up the channel, despite light rain showers, and when we turned the corner, heading north now toward Taku Glacier, conditions improved considerably. Merrill said he thought the ceiling was high enough over the glacier so that we could climb over it and on to the ice field. So up we went, just skimming over the two- or three-mile wide mass of crumpled blue ice that flowed down to the water between two high, rocky mountain walls. What a miserable place for a forced landing, I thought. I couldn't find one smooth area more than a few feet wide. At the top the ice gradually smoothed out, until we were soon flying over solid snow, broken only by an occasional sapphire-blue pond or the narrow small beginnings of what in a few months would become a vast network of dangerous crevasses.

A few more minutes of flying over the ice field and Merrill said he could see the area of the camp site, but that the actual camp was in the clouds. (The hut and tents are on a rocky promontory about 200 feet above the ice field, and the plane lands on the snow at its foot.) Merrill lowered his skis, and we circled once. The light was so flat that it was extremely difficult to tell just where the snow surface was,

but Merrill made a smooth landing, and Anne and I climbed
out into a world of white. No sign of any people, because
if they were sitting in the clouds they obviously weren't expecting us. A few moments later we heard great shouts and
watched several figures descending the rocky slope at break-
neck speed. One of them was our bearded daddy, and was
he surprised to see us! They had never dreamed that we
could make it up today. They had stood outside their tents,
catching glimpses of Merrill's plane through the fog, thinking
that he had absolutely lost his mind in trying to come up.

It was nice to get such a warm welcome — Anne was thoroughly enjoying everything but Daddy's bristly beard — that
she would have none of, and I can't say that I blamed her.
One of the men brought down a rucksack-type seat, like a
child's car chair. Anne climbed into it, Lowell lifted her
onto his back, and up we went, scrambling over rocks and
floundering into deep soft snow. At the top the mist was
breaking up so that we could see across the ice field for
miles, a vast plain of solid brilliant white, encircled by jagged
granite pinnacles, their tops disappearing into the cloud
layer. (Later on, when blue sky and sunshine took the place
of the clouds, the view was even more breathtaking.)

The camp consisted of a large tin hut, perched among
snow and big rocks, two small ones (a radio shack and an
outhouse), and eight little green tents sitting in the snow.
Between the tents and the largest hut was the "dining hall,"
a long wooden table and benches with an orange silk para-
chute used as an awning above. What a dash of vivid color
in the midst of so much white! Lowell took us on a tour before lunch, up a narrow path in the deep snow, where Anne
had a very difficult time walking, to the various tents. The
Frasers had one — Gretchen was one of the two women
there, one of our foremost woman skiers, the first American

woman to win an Olympic ski medal. Don, her husband, had also been on an Olympic team. The Haleys had another — Ted was one of Maynard Miller's scientists, and Peggy helped with the cooking. Then came Pepi and Franz Gabl, two Austrian brothers who are ski pros in our Far West. Then John Jay's tent, John Jay of ski movie fame — then Lowell and J.P. and Mike. The rest slept in bunks inside the main hut — L.T., Sr., Maynard, Dr. Nichols, and four other scientific men. Quite a gang for such a minute rock outcropping. "Camp Ten" had always been an all-male sanctuary, but Maynard really let down the barrier this year. He brought a guest book for the occasion and we all signed it, including Anne who scribbled over half a page.

The part of the camp that interested Anne the most was "Petunia," the little tin outhouse perched among rocks just below the main hut. If she made one trip, she must have made fifty! And I had to go with her each time because the "hole" was much too big for her, and I felt she could fall through. She was simply fascinated by the whole idea and wanted to stay right there in her "own little house."

Lunch consisted of dehydrated pea soup, cooked over a large primus stove, and canned chicken sandwiches. All the expedition members were taking turns cooking and washing dishes, and eating like kings — salmon, steak, chicken, fresh vegetables, strawberries, even watermelon! Their refrigerator was a big hole in the snow next to the outdoor table. A burlap cloth hung across the opening to keep out the mice. What persistent little animals, to find their way up there!

After lunch we all sat out on the rocks, in the hot sun, watching Merrill trying to find a crevasse from the air. The particular one which Lowell had used for a film sequence the day before was now covered with a ground fog. Merrill zoomed back and forth over the area, trying to find a hole to get down through. He finally landed out in the clear and taxied back under the cloud blanket. Mike and J.P. (who were in the plane) told us later that they couldn't locate the spot, that the plane had started to slip down an incline, and that they had to pile out and haul it back up with ropes. All in a day's work! They finally gave up and flew back to camp. Just then the fog lifted, and they were greeted with, "Now you can go back, it's clear."

Anne spent the afternoon, between trips to Petunia, washing clothes and dishes in a big dishpan on a bench outside the hut and playing "house" under the orange canopy. She might just as well have been home in her own back yard, though it was a little difficult for her to walk in the deep snow or scramble over the large rocks. I seriously considered staying overnight; we had been cordially invited, but I finally decided not to, mainly because the tent floors rested right on the snow and Lowell said everyone became miserably cold and damp while sleeping. This, despite two sleeping bags apiece. I wasn't sure if I could even get Anne into one, so that settled it. And Lowell was planning to return to Juneau the next day anyway. A wise decision in retrospect. Bad weather moved in as soon as we left and the camp was completely marooned for four straight days!

Instead of climbing back down the rocks to the airplane, Lowell skied down the front hill, with Anne on his back. I got down any way I could, usually sliding on my fanny. Merrill was waiting for us, and off we went, down over the glacier and around the corner. The weather seemed much better, so the trip was a pleasant half hour. It looked like things were breaking up, that we'd have clear weather again. Such a disappointment to wake up next morning and find ceiling and visibility zero again!

And four days later the weather was still miserable, but

Merrill thought he saw faint signs of clearing to the west, so he took off and disappeared around the bend. Anne and I waited at the airport a few hours, the weather improving slightly, but finally gave up and went into the little restaurant for lunch. When we came out, there were three heavily bearded men looking for us. A happy reunion, despite the beards, which were all shaved off the moment we reached the hotel, except Lowell's mustache, and that lasted overnight. It came off the next morning "by mutual consent."

We made one final side trip from Juneau down to Tracy Arm, one of the most spectacular fiords in the world, with an extremely active Sawyer glacier at the other end. The men were planning to fly down in a chartered Grumman Goose, meet a forestry boat waiting there for them, and take pictures from its decks of the great spectacle of falling ice. Just before they left, at seven in the morning, it suddenly dawned on us that there would be two extra seats on the plane, and that Anne and I could go along for the ride. They were to take off at eight, so it meant rushing frantically. Anne was so excited that she co-operated fully — a ride in one of those planes that we watched almost every day! Probably one of the highlights of the whole trip for her.

We took off just beyond the seaplane base and flew fairly low along the coast, past Taku Glacier. Then south, by steep, rocky mountain sides, cascading waterfalls, and an occasional glacier peeping out through a narrow gorge. A half hour later we turned left up one of the steepest and narrowest fiords (just barely room for the plane to turn around if it had to), high cliffs falling into turquoise blue water, dotted with little icebergs. We flew straight to the head of the fiord and banked steeply over the huge glacier there. It formed a wall several hundred feet above the water, and great chunks of ice were constantly falling with a loud roar. (Lowell said later that while they were there they also saw "calving" — icebergs being thrown up from underneath the water, with such intensity that the resulting huge waves threatened to overturn the little boat they were in.) They also watched massive cliffs of ice fall, making geysers of water hundreds of feet high. They hadn't expected so much ice activity, and Lowell had asked Merrill to fly over in his plane at a certain time, dropping some sticks of dynamite over the glacier to try to stir up some activity. It was too late to call him off, so he arrived at the appointed time and dropped the explosives, but the result was a complete fizzle: they all saw a faint pfft — pfft of white smoke and that was all.

We flew on down the ice-choked fiord (where we saw some hair seals on one large berg — there is a bounty on them because they eat the salmon) until we spotted the little green and yellow forestry boat. There were only a few scattered bergs, so we could land alongside. The men all got off into a little rowboat, while Anne and I waved good-by. How I would have loved to go along, but the boat just did not look big enough to hold all the men, plus a woman and a two-year-old child, for a full day.

If I had known what lay ahead of me on the ride back, I think I would have been content to perch on an iceberg near the boat for the rest of the day. The captain asked us to sit up in the co-pilot's seat, Anne in my lap, so we could see all about us. We took off into the fiord and I wondered when he would start turning around. I suddenly realized that he wasn't planning to, we were heading right for the mountain wall! We were climbing steeply, but it certainly didn't look to me as though we were going to make it. The cliffs were coming closer and closer, and I was getting more and more panicky. The pilot, calm and relaxed, applied more power, and we sailed easily over the top of the ridge. Whew! Throttling back, heading now along the coast line, he turned to me and asked if I had seen any mountain goats. No, I had not. "Would you mind if I flew closer to the mountains so we might spot some?" I was trapped. I could only mumble, "Fine," wondering what he meant by closer. I soon found out — we headed for the nearest rock wall, and I could pick out all the little wild flowers hiding among the stones before we finally peeled off and slipped over a pass. Still no goats, so we headed for the next mountain wall, and so on and on, until about ten mountain walls later Juneau was just beyond our nose, and we never did see that mountain goat. We landed smoothly on the water. Anne woke up, disappointed that the trip was over, and I mumbled my thanks to the captain for a pleasant ride.

The time had come to fly north. The weatherman gave us an excellent forecast for Sunday, so Lowell decided to fly up onto the icecap with Merrill first thing in the morning to get a couple of missing pictures. They'd return at eleven and we'd take off at noon. At eleven o'clock I was all packed and ready, but no Lowell. At twelve o'clock Anne and I ate our sandwiches in the hotel room. At one o'clock I really became concerned and called L.T., Sr. He was on his way out to the airport to catch his plane home, so we rode along with him, planning to find someone at the airfield who could take off and look for Lowell. (As I left the hotel, the CAA had had no word from them.) We all drove in strained silence, and imagine our tremendous relief when we saw Merrill's plane sitting on the ground! We found two sheepish men with quite a story: they had found a lovely flat mountaintop to land on, but the moment they set down, a cloud bank rolled in, so there they sat for a good hour, marooned in the clouds. Of course they just plain forgot to report in to the CAA.

I was a wreck, Anne was exhausted, and the two wayward fliers were tired, too, so we all mutually agreed to postpone our departure until after a good night's sleep. Would we ever be leaving Juneau?

CHAPTER VI

Anchorage and the
Statehood Celebration

Oᴜʀ two planes took off early Monday morning, June 23rd, but Merrill was alone in his, because J.P. and Mike were staying behind to finish up odds and ends, including filming the commercial. We had a five-hour flight ahead of us that day, a kind of detour inland, finally turning west to hit the coast at Anchorage, actually flying over Canada most of the time. We had to fly this way because the CAA frowns on small planes flying the coastal route — rugged, uncharted mountains, no place to land, and treacherous weather. Certainly all right by me!

We flew up the coast to Haines, a small seaport founded by Presbyterian missionaries. And then over the old Indian village of Klukwan. Many years ago, the proud warlike Chilcat tribe (a branch of the Tlingits) made this their main home. They were famous for their magnificent blankets woven from the long hair of mountain goats and beautifully dyed and decorated with religious symbols. Few of these Indians remain there today, and unfortunately they have given up blanket weaving. Then inland, following a long wide valley, another route blazed by the gold-seeking forty-niners and called the Dalton Trail, now dotted with only an occasional tiny settlement — mostly isolated prospectors' cabins. Low, tundra-covered mountains rose on either side of this valley, reminding us of the Scottish Highlands we had visited some years ago, and far to our left we caught glimpses through the clouds of the world's highest coastal mountains — the St. Elias range. Mount St. Elias is 18,008 feet, and its neighbor, Mt. Logan, is 19,850 feet, the second highest peak on the North American continent. They rise straight from the sea, part of a virtually unexplored, uninhabited 300-mile coast line.

Merrill was usually just behind us, and several times we both had to descend a few thousand feet beneath the clouds of little rain showers. We kept in constant touch by radio — once I called to him that my pilot was asleep, and could he tell me just where we were? A few moments later Anne wanted lunch, so I nudged Lowell awake and passed the controls back to him. He immediately called Merrill, saying, "That was one of the shortest naps I ever had." Merrill must have gotten hungry at the same moment because he called back, "I have four packages of pickles, did you get any at all?" Such trivial radio conversations, but what a comfort to have company over that wild terrain. Actually the flight today was far easier and less spectacular than some of those we had undertaken earlier, so we all relaxed a bit more, although Anne never slept a wink. She read or played the full five hours, with never a whimper or complaint.

We broke the trip after three hours of flying by landing at Northway. I can't quite call it a town, it's just a CAA

station, with several shacks and radio towers, plus eight
homes, a small general store and post office, and even smaller
"hotel." Several wives and children of CAA men came up
to visit with us after we landed. They said they liked living
there, that their tour of duty was two years, with ten weeks
paid vacation each year. I asked about the children and
their schooling. They said there were fifteen youngsters in
the town and so the CAA supplied schoolhouse and teacher.

The small hotel was like a cozy home — a big kitchen where
we all congregated, a little dining room with one long table,
and four bedrooms. All as neat as a pin and run by the friendly,
pleasant grandparents of one of the young couples. (The
granddaddy was vacuuming when we came in.) A cheery
sight which almost always welcomed us in the kitchens of
Alaskan homes was the large, ever-hot coffee pot sitting on the
stove. No matter what the time of day, everyone was always
ready to stop and "have another cup."

We would have liked to stay on in Northway — the countryside was beautiful and the people were friendly, but we
were still the Cheechakoes (newcomers) of the North and
always in a hurry. We stopped only long enough for some
lunch, gas for *Charlie*, and a little fun for Anne on one of
the children's swings. Then we had a fairly short flight left,
turning west, across low mountains paralleling the great
ranges. We had to stay under 6000 feet, skimming over the
terrain and bouncing about because flying any higher with
no flight plan would inevitably bring on those ever-vigilant
jet interceptors. One had to ask for a special clearance above
that altitude. The air force plays a most important role. Almost constantly, no matter where we went in Alaska, we could
hear the jets zooming about at high altitudes above us.

Most of the snow-covered mountains of the Wrangell and
Chugach ranges to our left were in the clouds, their glaciers

winding down to the valleys beneath us — glaciers that don't compare in beauty with those around Juneau. The lower areas are covered with black dirt and gravel, the debris which the ice has pushed down the mountainside and then left as the glacier recedes. Suddenly we spotted some of those elusive white mountain sheep on a nearby rocky pinnacle, the first we'd seen on our trip so far, but they are supposed to be all over this particular area.

Soon the valley beneath us widened, and we saw signs of farming. A few small fields here and there first, then a broad level floor of large green and brown squares. The Matanuska Valley, Alaska's biggest and one of its finest farm areas. We had heard that vegetables and dairy products produced there rivaled the best of any in the other states, and we were looking forward to finding out just how these farmers of the Far North pulled off such a feat. We could now see the large city of Anchorage ahead of us, on a point of land jutting out into the Cook Inlet. However, we couldn't fly straight toward it, but had to hug the mountains to the south instead, because of the highly strategic Elmendorf Air Force Base just ahead.

Once around that formidable obstacle, we came in over the city and landed at a tiny dirt air strip just on the other side. We picked this airport instead of the big International Field because of the location of the Cessna distributor. And in order to park right in front of his workshop, we had to taxi *Charlie* across a main road, over railroad tracks, and down two dirt roads! All routine here, apparently, as there were several planes ahead of us.

Any traveler's first impression of Anchorage (other than the obvious fact that it is a large modern city) must be that it is also home for countless airplanes, big and little. Alaska is the land of light plane flying, and the three civilian

airfields of Anchorage were literally covered with them. At
Lake Hood, the seaplane base behind the Cessna hangar, sea-
planes were moored to every foot of its shore line, and there
was a four-year wait for tie-down space!

Whenever we flew about in the area we felt as if we were
dodging traffic on Highway No. 1. And at five o'clock each
evening the line-up for the runways was like a wartime
queue. We gathered that many people commuted to their
jobs in the city from outlying areas. We also learned that
many Anchorage families went off together on weekends,
flying their little "puddle jumpers" to nearby cabins or camps
for hunting, fishing, or swimming.

So we weren't overly amazed when the Civil Aeronautics
Office in Alaska told us that there were 2000 active certified
pilots in the state, out of a civilian population of 130,000
(not including natives). That's the same as saying one in
every sixty-five persons in Chattanooga, Tennessee, or Sac-
ramento, California, owns an active pilot's license!

Anchorage is also a major center for airline activities:
an important refueling stop for many international planes,
and local airlines radiate out from there all over Alaska. The
Reeve Aleutian Airways has to deal with what probably is the
toughest flying weather in the world and, at the same time,
has one of the best safety records. They service the stormy,
inevitably fogbound Aleutians. Pacific Northern Airlines flies
south to Seattle, Northwest stops there en route to the Orient,
and KLM, Air France, and SAS touch down on polar flights
between Europe and the Orient. All this international aviation activity has helped make the immense new International
Airport one of the largest and busiest in the world.

Leaving *Charlie* among many fellow Cessnas, we drove
toward the heart of the city, through miles of drive-in dinettes,
motels, bars, gas stations, bowling alleys, trailer parks, and

supermarkets — all liberally sprinkled with neon signs. We could easily be back in any large sprawling city near home. A city of 40,000 residents, we were told, one seventh of Alaska's population. The local Chamber of Commerce proudly states that the population of the greater Anchorage area has had the largest growth (percentagewise) of any city in North America during the past ten years. At the expense of losing the charm and beauty of a smaller town, I thought. I would like to have seen it when it was the construction headquarters for the building of the Alaska Railroad in 1914. The small boats which used nearby Ship Creek as an "anchorage" gave the town its name. There were only 3700 people in Anchorage just before World War II, so the biggest growth has come since then.

In the center of town many tall buildings — 14-story apartment houses and hotels — rise up from the flat peninsula against the snow-covered Chugach Mountain background in the distance. The biggest surprise to me was the view from our twelfth-floor hotel-room window. Looking north across the blue waters of Cook Inlet, we could see snow-covered Mount McKinley, over 120 miles away, to me a shimmering mirage because of its seeming aloneness and its great height, rising abruptly from the plain.

Anchorage was our base of operations for the next two weeks, and when we weren't on junkets to outlying areas, Anne and I wandered about the city itself. Our first sightseeing day was a hot one — a cloudless blue sky and eighty-degree temperatures. So the natural spot to head for was Lake Spenard, Anchorage's summer playground. The soft sand beach was covered with bronze sun bathers and more were splashing about in the clear warm water.

On other such days we drove out among the modern suburbs, Spenard, East Chester, Mountain View, and others —

quiet, tree-lined streets, attractive modern homes with neat
little lawns and a liberal sprinkling of spring flowers. Houses
tend to be smaller because it costs more than double to build
there than elsewhere in the states. Most building materials are
imported by ship or plane from great distances. Also, plumbers
get $8.50 per hour and carpenters get twelve dollars!

Anchorage's average temperature in the summer is fifty-
seven degrees, so we did have cool days, too — cloudy and
rainy weather when the temperatures dropped into the low
fifties, and we had to dig into our suitcases for our woolen
suits and sweaters.

Those were the days we spent roaming around the city
itself, shopping, running errands, and just plain looking about.
Our little guidebook told us that we would find four radio
broadcasting stations, two TV stations, three theaters, two
large modern hospitals, twenty-six churches, and department
stores and small specialty shops by the score. We found the
stores all right, (leave it to the women, was Lowell's re-
mark), but quickly discovered that prices were at least twice
as high as those back home. In one elegant dress shop a sales-
lady commented on my good sun tan (obtained through
Charlie's windshield, I guess). But Anne had another explanation — "Mummie's been out in the midnight sun."

Whenever we used the restaurants (some were among the
finest we had ever visited) we were also forcefully reminded
of the high cost of living. In fact, it was a great shock at
breakfast the first morning to discover that orange juice, bacon,
eggs, toast, and coffee cost each of us $2.50. An even greater
blow came at dinnertime when soup, hamburgers, and milk
shakes for two came to $4.50! Highway robbery — but under-
standable when one realizes that much of the food is imported
by air. And, fortunately for the Alaskans, wages are on the
same high scale.

One day in Anchorage that we will never forget began, as usual, with shopping and sightseeing in the morning. After lunch, Lowell drove out to a local forestry farm, on the lookout for more baby animals. (I had had enough of them!) Anne and I went back to our room for a rest. Our window looked out on a back alley, but just beyond a low building we could see the main street and the Federal Building (a combination courthouse and post office).

At two-fifteen the fire siren suddenly went off — it was mounted on a rooftop just to our left, so it was an ear-splitting wail to us, and it went on and on and on. I thought I knew right away what it meant and rushed to the window. People quickly gathered at the street corners and car horns started blowing. There was still a look of uncertainty on people's faces (mine included). As the car horns grew in volume and the whistle kept going, incredibility took over. Then when the church bells chimed in with "My country, 'tis of thee," everyone knew for certain that statehood had just been passed by Congress! Now the joyous celebrating began in earnest.

The crowds at the four main street corners became enormous within minutes and the main street jammed with cars, all honking their horns. I noticed a lot of activity on the roof of the Federal Building — five or six men pulling a long roll of red, white, and blue material from a large box, then dropping it down over the front parapet. This was too much — I had to go see what was going on. Lowell had told us to stick by the phone until we heard from him about the animal farm, but this was too big a day just to sit in a hotel room.

So off we dashed, Anne still holding her ears for fear the whistle might blast off again. When we arrived in front of the Federal Building, I saw the explanation for the bunting —

a huge American flag had been unfurled, covering most of the long, three-story high building. And just as we arrived, a shiny red fire truck pulled up to the curb in front and sent its long ladder up and over to the field of stars. Then a lovely young lady in black slacks ("Queen of the Fur Rendezvous," we learned later), followed by a fireman, climbed slowly up the long ladder and pinned a large glittering silver star among the other forty-eight. Everyone cheered, and then came the mad scramble of amateur and professional picture takers. Everybody in Anchorage had to have his or her picture taken in front of that flag — self-conscious mothers, reluctant children, eager, pretty teen-agers. And it was impossible to tell the few professionals from the many amateurs, as I have never seen such elaborate equipment. Most people had one or two expensive still cameras, and many had movie equipment — a few complete with tripod! I decided to join right in and made Anne stand in front of the flag, holding up a copy of the newspaper "extra" (newsboys were already yelling "Extra" up and down the street). The headlines were eight inches high and said, "We're in."

We sat on the steps of the Federal Building for another hour, watching the wild goings on. Rolls of toilet paper were being unfurled from an upstairs window; firecrackers were exploding all about us; a TV camera was interviewing people just across the street; and of course the cars were still parading by, bumper to bumper, their horns blaring. The most amusing sight of all was a huge stuffed moose being pulled down the street by a truck — a large sign on its back read: "Look out Texas, I'm the biggest bull now!"

It was thrilling to be part of such a momentous event. We had come to Alaska, anticipating statehood, but we found, as we traveled about, that while most people were for it, the general feeling was that it was still in the future, that it would be postponed again. So we, and most of Anchorage, too, were in for a very pleasant surprise.

For weeks local residents, with great hopes, had been building a mammoth pile of timbers and logs and old railroad ties in the middle of a park near the center of town — "the largest bonfire Alaska had ever seen," so the papers claimed, to be lit if statehood should come through. It was touched off at eight o'clock that night, amid throngs of celebrating Alaskans, while all the church bells rang out with patriotic songs. I could see the glow from our hotel window, even though a five-story building blocked a direct view. (Anne was asleep, worn out from the earlier celebration, and I had had no luck in finding a baby sitter.) By ten o'clock I was beginning to wish the bedlam would die down — the noise of the car horns was deafening and the shouting and the singing almost as loud. When we finally dared to open a window, around 1 A.M., someone started throwing big firecrackers just beneath us, and it was impossible to sleep. That awakened Anne and it was a long while before she settled down again. The city was filled with bleary-eyed people the next day!

CHAPTER VII

We Visit a Farmer
in Matanuska Valley

Despite the lack of sleep, we were up early the following morning and took off at nine o'clock. We had only a twenty-five minute flight that day (about fifty miles), and we were retracing our steps, hugging the Chugach Mountains, past Elmendorf Air Force Base, and up the famed Matanuska Valley, those brown and green squares lying between the Chugach and Talkeetna Mountains. We were headed for Palmer, the principal town in the area, a major stop for the Alaska Railroad, en route to Fairbanks from Anchorage, and the Richardson Highway, the link between Anchorage and the Alaska Highway that we had followed north.

As with most other areas in Alaska, the valley was first discovered when gold was found in the Talkeetna Mountains in the late 1800s. This particular gold rush was a small one, however, and it wasn't until 1911 that the first handful of white settlers came in to homestead. They were mostly trappers, fishermen, and miners. In 1916, when the Alaska Railroad was built through the valley, mining of gold and coal really grew in importance. Farming took a lot longer to develop beyond a few isolated homesteads.

In 1929 the management of the Alaska Railroad made the first organized effort to settle farmers there. They brought in about a hundred families, but very few of them are left today. In 1935 our federal government decided to try group settlement as a part of the Federal Emergency Administration of Public Works. Settlers were picked from the northern Midwest, where farming conditions are similar to those in the Matanuska, and 200 families arrived from Seattle in 1935. But large government-settlement schemes were abandoned as the first did not turn out successfully. Poor selection of colonists, inadequacy of the forty-acre lots for commercial agriculture, and underdeveloped markets caused all but about thirty to leave. Then individual homesteading families took over, especially after World War II, when a number of ex-servicemen and their families (often soldiers who had seen duty in Alaska and had fallen in love with the rugged, beautiful area, or those ready to escape humdrum daily life back home for the rigors of the frontier) took advantage of the veteran benefits of the Homestead Act. This law states that "qualified persons may acquire up to 160 acres of land by living on it for three years and by building a habitable house and bringing at least ¹⁄₁₆th of the area under cultivation by the end of the third year. . . ." Veterans are allowed more leniency in the residency requirement.

Actually, many Alaskans we talked with felt this act is too restrictive and should be amended to help promote land settlement. Some felt that 160 acres wasn't enough and hindered the development of agriculture on a bigger scale. And there are a lot more hidden restrictions than just 160 acres. The biggest problem is how to clear this land, which is often forested and usually far from good roads. The cost of a bulldozer is staggering — land clearing costs $150 to $200 per acre. Also, livestock, feed, freight, and living costs are considerably higher than elsewhere in the states. A potential homesteader needs capital before he can even start to homestead, and it is usually a good while before he can make his land pay off. So don't go West, young man, unless you have money in your pocket, a knowledge of farming, and plenty of fortitude and patience. Alaska also highly recommends that you have a temporary home all lined up (don't forget, living costs are staggering!) and a temporary, part-time job to tide you over until your crops begin paying dividends. You still want to go?

Well, we visited just such a couple who took the gamble and had it pay off. We landed at a grass strip in Palmer, were met by J.P. and Mike in a Hertz car, and drove on up the valley to the northernmost farm. Darrell Callison had been a B–17 pilot in World War II. His home was on his family's farm in West Virginia. He saved most of his pay, and after the war he and his wife, who was a nurse, came to Alaska as homesteaders, staking out their claim in the northern section of the Matanuska. They lived in a tent from June until September that first year while they cleared ground together and built a small log cabin. Then came five years of backbreaking work on the land, and part-time jobs — in a mine for him and in a hospital for her. They still work hard, but what a life they have made for themselves! Their home sits high on a hillside, with a beautiful view of the Matanuska River below and the mountains beyond. They have a lovely front lawn bordered by gigantic mountain ash and aspen trees. They have roses and peonies in flower beds by the house and a large plastic swimming pool for their two children. The house itself couldn't be more attractive — it's made of log (part of the original structure), but they have painted the logs brown, and the house has a green trim, so it's far from the rough stage. The interior is just as attractive, with every single bit done by themselves. The walls are plastered and painted, and there are two bedrooms, one with bunk beds for the two boys who are five and two, a lovely large living room, complete with television set and picture window, and a kitchen which is the most modern imaginable. Besides the electric stove and refrigerator, there is an entire shelf of assorted electric cookers.

We all enjoyed being with the family. The husband and wife are the finest of people, and the little boys are well behaved and fun loving. Anne had the time of her life with Lynn, the oldest. They played together all day long, and when both grew tired of chasing each other about on the lawn, they settled down on the couch together to watch a children's television show — the same one Anne sees every evening at home.

We spent the morning out in the fields taking pictures. Darrell is a truck farmer, raising lettuce, cabbage, radishes, and other vegetables. He had only twenty-five acres under cultivation because that is all the market can absorb at the moment. But he still makes a good income — last year the most successful farmers in the valley cleared around $20,000.

The Callisons have to work very hard during the summer months — she works in the fields, too, and they had four hired women picking radishes the day of our visit. Although their growing season is short, there are so many hours of sunlight in the summer (nineteen, to be exact) that there is a real danger of produce "overgrowing." In other words, if they don't pick all the vegetables within a couple of days after they first become ripe, they grow too big and pulpy and spoil quickly.

We watched the large red radishes being picked, the most beautiful I have ever seen, and then brought into a big root cellar which had an elaborate built-in cooling system. They were dunked into huge bins of cold water, then tied into bunches, and stored overnight in bins. The next morning Darrell would truck them to Anchorage to the Piggly Wiggly Market.

For any interested farmers, efficient growers in the Matanuska area usually gets yields of twelve tons of cabbage, seven tons of lettuce, and seven tons of carrots to the acre. Dairying there is just as successful (Alaska cows yield more milk per head than the national average), the most important enterprise in the area, and potatoes rank second, amounting to about $1,000,000 farm value annually. In other words, the products are varied and of exceptional quality, despite the rigors of the climate. And Mother Nature does pose formidable problems. Aside from the short summer growing season (approximately 100 days), moose can cause damage to fences, bears can attack cattle, severe winter winds can cause considerable erosion, and the heavy spring runoff can do the same. The winters are severe, but not as tough as one imagines for an area so close to the Arctic Circle. The floor of Matanuska Valley is covered with snow all winter, which helps insulate the plants (such as Mrs. Callison's peonies and rosebushes). The temperature averages around ten degrees, and there are about six hours of daylight in December, the darkest month. The Callisons don't seem to mind it, and the health of their children doesn't seem to suffer in the least. They (like many other Alaskans) plan an annual six-week trip south to other states during the worst of the winter.

We were most interested in one of Mother Nature's biggest obstacles — *permafrost*, perennially frozen ground which underlines most of Alaska. However, we discovered this is not much of a problem south of the Alaska Range. The Matanuska Valley has many feet of topsoil covering the deeper frozen ground. North of the Alaska Range, except for a few feet of topsoil thawed each summer, permafrost ranges from one to several hundred feet deep. (The big problems posed by permafrost north of the Alaska Range are impeded surface drainage — we sloshed through many acres of summer puddles north of the Arctic Circle — and the difficulties involved in digging beneath the surface. In the northern towns pipes are usually laid above the ground, and most houses have foundation troubles — they tilt at various angles because of the uneven thawing and freezing of the ice just beneath.)

Mother Nature isn't the only cause of the problems facing farmers. Alaska is capable of growing at least half of the food for the present population, but less than one fifth is supplied at the moment. The state government says, "Long-established buying patterns give way slowly as local products replace stateside imports." We were told by the local people that during World War II, when farm outputs first began to grow to any importance, the Armed Forces in Alaska bought up all local produce and the citizens had to turn to outside markets. Once the war was over, they just didn't want to change their habits. Today Alaska is importing ninety-five per cent of her meat, seventy per cent of her milk, and eighty-five per cent of her fresh produce. Of course, there will always be many foodstuffs that Alaskans will have to import (as in almost any other state), and the produce from the farms will be highly subject to seasons. One city housewife told me she preferred canned or powdered milk to fresh because in the winter the latter was so often delivered frozen.

(Only thirty per cent of the milk consumed now comes from local dairies.)

The moral of the story? If you're sick of your job in an overcrowded city in one of the other states, don't just pull up stakes and move to an Alaskan farm! First, make sure you have plenty of capital, farming know-how, the will to work hard, and an awareness of the numerous obstacles in your path. If, then, you are still all set to go, good for you, and lots of luck!

CHAPTER VIII

Other Alaskan Inhabitants — and a
Bush Pilot with a Unique Invention

BEFORE flying on to the north, Lowell and
Merrill took time out to locate an area thickly populated by
the great Alaska brown bears, and their ensuing adventures
were responsible for a few more gray hairs on all heads, especially mine! Their first stop was McNeil River, and a small
Wildlife Service camp there, on the virtually uninhabited
Cook Peninsula, southwest of Anchorage. But the area had
no air strip and no place for a float plane to land on the
river itself. The only alternative was to arrive at dead low
tide and use the protruding hard-packed sand bars. To time
this just right they had to take off from Anchorage at three
in the morning. It was cloudy and rainy, I noticed, as I
peeked out the window — no more sleep for me that night
either. Lowell told me later that the flight was one of the
most hair-raising he had ever taken. The clouds hovered at
400 feet, so the two planes sped along at treetop level. The

visibility was poor, with rain showers making it worse. Lowell was most uneasy, but thought Merrill knew what he was doing, so stuck right to his tail. It turned out later that Merrill was most uneasy, too! They had to drop lower and lower, but were above the waters of the Cook Inlet. They found themselves looking up to the trees on the sandy bank, and worse yet, they were being tossed about by a tremendous wind, a phenomenon for which the area is widely known. The winds were so strong that when they flew past a waterfall, Lowell noticed the water was going up instead of down!

He began to worry about the coming landing on the short, narrow sand bar, doubly complicated by such a wind. Merrill was concerned, too, but being a bush pilot of vast experience with the gravel bars in the Far North, he decided to give it a try. Lowell watched him go in, touch his wheels down at the water's edge, race across the short bar, and stop abruptly at the far end, his wheels at the water's edge. At that moment, Lowell decided that since he had never landed on a sand bar before, this was not the time to try. The problem was that while Merrill carried the two passengers, J.P. and Mike, Lowell had all their supplies, a vital consideration in view of the complete isolation of the area. The Wildlife man, Ivan Marks, was the only local inhabitant, living in an aluminum hut (to discourage his four-legged neighbors) with just enough supplies to keep himself going through the whole summer period. So J.P. and Mike were about to be stranded for twenty-four hours, if not longer, what with the unpredictable weather in the area. Lowell decided to air drop some of the unbreakable bundles, shoving them out the door at the right moment over the bar. A tricky operation, considering the strong wind and water on four sides of the target area. But Lowell saw no great splashes and decided all was going well, until he received a radio call from Merrill:

"Hey, what's the idea? That d—— tripod just missed my airplane by two feet!" So Lowell called a halt to his aerial supply operation. He watched Merrill make a hair-raising take-off, barely staggering back into the air while being buffeted by those strong winds. Then the two quickly turned north and headed straight for Anchorage.

They spent the rest of the day back in our hotel, pacing the floor and calling the Weather Bureau. Luckily for them, the weather cleared that evening, and they were off again at three the next morning. The next twenty-four hours, Lowell said later, were probably the most exciting of the entire trip for him. This time they both landed safely on the sand bar and joined the two other men. Ivan Marks led them to a nearby stream teeming with salmon and virtually surrounded by the great Alaska brown bears. The thousands of fish were leaping, wiggling, and splashing their way upstream to spawn, and the bears were all congregating at the water's edge for their annual gluttonous feast. Ivan assured the men that they could set up their cameras and photograph the huge carnivorous animals in relative safety. Mr. Bear was too intent on his meal of fish. The warden stood by them with a cocked gun, just in case. Lowell said later that the great bears passed within twenty or thirty feet of the men, and one or two took the time to turn and growl, but then went on. Ivan said he could tell by their ears what their thoughts were. If the bear's ears stayed up, he might growl in indignation but then continue to his feast. If his ears went back, the warden would have to fire immediately — the bear was about to charge, and from such a short distance one can't wait even one second.

Fortunately for all concerned, no ears did go back, and the men spent the entire day in that precarious position, obtaining some of the finest bear pictures ever filmed. The

big creatures jumped and dived into the water like awkward
clowns, splashing about and chasing the fish all over the
stream. There were so many salmon that one snap of the
powerful jaws (contrary to popular belief, bears don't scoop
out fish with their huge paws, but grab them directly with
their mouths) usually produced results, and once the bears
had their fill of fish, they merely went for the roe, slashing
the salmon open to look for it. They left the dying fish on
the rocks for the swarms of screaming sea gulls hopping
about beside them.

The men were most grateful to Ivan, without whose help
they could never have gotten such pictures. He is one of the
few who understand these enigmatic animals, but even he
was fooled by his gigantic neighbors. A few days later he
accompanied a still photographer to the same spot and was
severely mauled by an unpredictable female.

With the bear pictures safely in film cans on their way
back to New York, we turned our thoughts to the north now,
toward McKinley Park, then to Fairbanks, and later above
the Arctic Circle to our final goal in the rugged Brooks
Range.

Early on the morning of July 4th, we all met out at the
airfield, with our mountains of bags and equipment. Our
only holiday celebration was the setting off of one giant
firecracker. Lowell secretly tossed it over behind the men
while they were loading their plane. It came as a great surprise, and we all had a good laugh, but the biggest laugh
was on Lowell, for the exploding powder threw up a small
stone, scratching him on the arm. "That's what you get,"
they all said.

We split up that day — Merrill's plane flying non-stop north
to Fairbanks to pick up film supplies, while we took *Charlie*
at a more leisurely pace, landing at Talkeetna, en route to

McKinley Park. Our northerly heading was not difficult to find
— we merely pointed the plane's nose toward that gigantic
white mountain over 120 miles straight north of us. We
climbed out over the northern arm of the Cook Inlet, and over
the mouth of the Susitna River directly ahead. We followed
the river (and the Alsaka Railroad tracks going to Fairbanks)
all the way to Talkeetna, flying low over the flat, wooded
valley floor. The rugged, rocky 8000-foot Talkeetna Mountains rose to our right, while the snow-covered Alaska Range
towered up on the horizon to our left.

The many small ponds and lakes beneath us were favorite
hunting and fishing hide-outs for outdoor-minded Anchorage
residents. We spotted some of the cabins, almost hidden
beneath towering virgin timber. We even saw a few float
planes sitting on the still waters of some of the lakes. From
our low altitude we also saw many moose and a few huge
brown bears looking for food in the numerous small meadows
or standing by the countless little streams. Some stampeded
at the sound of *Charlie's* engine, but others stood still, apparently used to being buzzed from above.

On north above the valley we flew, passing the tiny river
settlements of Caswell, Montana, and Fish Lake. Talkeetna
was next, with maybe ten log and frame houses instead of the
usual five. I spotted the CAA's good asphalt runway just to the
east of the river and town, but Lowell was already circling
the local bush pilot's private grass strip — what looked like a
short narrow front lawn to me, enclosed by buildings and wires
at one end and the riverbank on the other. I just closed my
eyes and wondered at the courage of Alaskan bush pilots.
This one in particular, Don Sheldon, is nationally known for
his daring missions supplying and rescuing climbers on nearby
Mount McKinley. Lowell had heard about these feats and was
thinking of a possible tie-in with our filming.

So in we came, Lowell exhibiting all the skill of his bush-pilot friends. As we taxied toward the homemade, corrugated iron hangar, out loped tall lanky Don himself, all arms and legs, a broad open smile on his handsome face. A friendly, good-natured clown was my first impression — hard to believe he was a crack pilot, too. Don, thirty-six years old, came from Wyoming in 1938 and now runs six planes out of Talkeetna.

I knew right away that Anne and I were in for a long morning's wait as the two men immediately launched into a discussion of one of Don's newest projects — shooting wolves with guns attached to the wing struts of his Piper Super Cruiser airplane. (Each wolf brings a forty-dollar bounty.) Lowell was thinking of working in this area in another few weeks, using Talkeetna as a base, so here was my chance to scout around the town, especially the local hotel. We didn't have far to go — just a few yards beyond the end of the runway! The main street of Talkeetna, a dusty dirt road, ran at a ninety-degree angle to the little runway and was enclosed by eight or ten log and frame buildings, the "inn" the only two-story one. Anne and I walked into its front entrance, saw a dark, smoky poolroom on the left (filled with men, and it was Friday morning) and an equally dark and crowded barroom on the right. We climbed the steep rickety stairs just ahead of us and found four bedrooms at the top. All their doors were open, so I could see four unmade beds and men's clothing scattered all over. The bathroom, which Anne wanted to visit (of course), was littered with shaving brushes and men's lotions. Obviously bachelor's quarters and not the place for us!

We beat a hasty retreat back to the runway and walked down a little gravel path along one side. It led us to a small log cabin in the midst of a clearing, surrounded by a vegetable and flower garden. Nothing unusual about that sight in Alaska, but when I took a closer look at the cabin, which was painted white with green trim, I realized it was certainly different from any we had yet seen. The entire house seemed covered with flowers! There were marigolds and petunias in beds around the foundation, rosebushes at the four corners, a flowering vine climbing up the trellis framing the doorway, little bronze pots of pansies and forget-me-nots hanging at various levels by the door, and red geraniums peeping out from between red and white gingham curtains at the windows. I just stood and stared at such a lovely scene and didn't realize that someone could be in the house, staring back at me.

Barely a moment after we paused, the door flew open and a short, dark-haired matronly woman came rushing out to smother us with affectionate greetings. Obviously we were strangers in town, and could we come in for a cup of that inevitably ready Alaskan coffee? I was eager to see inside such an attractive exterior, and also Anne was beginning to display the two-year-old's talent for picking every flower in sight. So before any major damage could be done, I whisked her inside.

The interior was just as attractive, with polished log walls, gleaming wood floors covered with thick, black bear rugs, a great stone fireplace, whose many small, smooth, colored rocks had been waxed to shine almost like jewels, and extra-large, comfortable sofas and armchairs. The kitchen area was along the right wall as we went in, the fireplace on the left, and bedroom furniture toward the rear of the long one-room cabin. Anne made a beeline for the fur rugs, while our hostess and I took chairs by the fireplace. She was eager to chat and told me this was her first year in Talkeetna, that she had come from Wyoming to be the only teacher in the local school. But she was a writer at heart, she said, indicating a battered old typewriter, and then launched into a long soliloquy on statehood issues and subsequent problems. I would have loved to learn more about her and her life there, but couldn't change the subject.

A short while later I glanced out the window and noticed Lowell and Don about to get into the Piper Cruiser. So I thanked the friendly woman and then rushed outside to find out what was up now. More delay? Lowell and Don were going to give the wolf-hunting mechanism a tryout. While flying along the river, Lowell would toss out some empty five-gallon gas tins. Then Don would descend to about fifty feet and shoot at them. The four twelve-gauge shotguns were fastened to the two struts, and he had set his big sight above the instrument panel inside (the smaller one was welded onto the cowling on the nose outside). Don had added four switches near his stick, which he flipped to fire the guns, either separately or simultaneously.

It looked as if we would be in town another two hours anyway, and Anne was beginning to whine and complain. So I got our box lunch out of *Charlie* (the one we were to eat while en route) and we walked down to the river's edge, at the foot of the runway. We found a lovely sandy beach for our picnic and also had a front-row seat for the aerial "strafing exhibition."

We finally left Talkeetna at 2:00 P.M., heading north again, along the river, toward McKinley Park. The flat, forested land to our left is one of the areas now being developed into farming by homesteaders. (Some of the much publicized "fifty-niners" from Detroit later settled here. Don Sheldon was to become their only contact with the outside world.) The rest of the flight was relatively easy and uneventful. Mount McKinley, to our left, was hidden in the clouds, so the only other diversion was the little settlements along the river beneath us. Groups of four or five cabins clustered together, with the most outlandish names — Gold Creek, Colorado, Hurricane, Honolulu, Windy, and Lagoon. Perhaps named by settlers from the balmier fiftieth state, or those who wished they were there instead! The river finally petered out into many little streams, and the single-track railroad and the Denali Highway (actually only a dirt road), coming in from the Richardson Highway, swung toward the northwest. We noted another, wider dirt road heading north and followed that. Lowell quickly realized our mistake and turned back to pick up the railroad again. The road we had followed was labeled "sled road" on our map and probably headed toward the mining camps in the mountains due north of us. Beyond the rim of the main towns and cities of Alaska, there just aren't roads or railroads to follow when flying about the state, other than the railroad between Anchorage and Fairbanks, the Denali Highway connecting McKinley Park with the other highways, the Glenn Highway and Richardson Highway connecting Anchorage and Valdez with the main Alaska Highway coming in from Canada to Fairbanks. Alaskans are confident of tremendous development within their state in the next ten years, but this northern region we were approaching may take a lot longer. The land of the permafrost, where, except for a foot or two of topsoil, the ground remains frozen all year long. No big trees beneath us any more, just small aspen and stunted pine and low, green bushes covering most of the hills — the famous tundra of the world's far northern regions. Mile after mile of this as far as we could see, topped by the snow and rock mountains in the distance, crisscrossed by glacial streams with wide sand bars and dotted with countless small ponds and lakes.

This is also the land of the caribou and the Dall sheep. The latter live among the lower mountains (which were on our right) during the long hard winter, have their babies there in the early spring, then migrate across the valley in June to spend the summer in the higher Alaska mountain range (to our left). Most of this migration was already over the spring we arrived — only a few isolated herds left, some of which we spotted from the air.

The caribou are the nomads of the north, constantly on the move. They follow the ancient trails of their ancestors, stopping only briefly to graze, constantly looking for new feeding grounds. They are primarily animals of the tundra, but their constant search also takes them into the mountains and forests.

And this is the home of the grizzly bears, but they were hard to find as they stick pretty much to the thickets during the daytime. We saw more moose from the air than any other animal.

The railroad and road led us through a narrow pass between two low mountains, and then just ahead we spotted the railroad station for McKinley Park and the brown hotel building nearby. We descended rapidly and came down low over the daily train to land on a good gravel strip running parallel to the tracks. We had arrived at one of the great tourist meccas in Alaska.

CHAPTER IX

McKinley Park — a Luxury Hotel
and a Wilderness Camp

T HE McKinley Park Hotel (put up by the Department of the Interior) is probably one of the ugliest buildings ever built — a two-story high, long, brown, barnlike structure. But we found the interior attractive and comfortable. All the waiters and waitresses in the large dining room were college students, which contributed considerably to the friendly, informal atmosphere.

Unlike most hotels, the guests there were all transients, staying a day or two at the most. Anne and I remained four days, while Lowell went on a photographic reconnaissance trip up into the Brooks Range. Watching the rapid turnover of tourists each day, I began to feel like a permanent fixture. For the most part, the visitors were on tours, with each moment well regulated for them. There were carefully marked nature walks of one-, two-, or three-mile length, or a twelve-hour bus ride through the park (McKinley Park is second in size only to Yellowstone, with an area of over 300 square miles), which left the hotel at four in the morning. But a two-and-a-half-year-old simply cannot be regulated to that extent, so there was very little to keep her occupied in such grown-up surroundings. At first she tried to make friends with the tame squirrels around the hotel, but the moment she tried to reach out and pet them, they raced away, down into the nearest hole. She quickly grew exasperated with her cautious little friends, and when we went down to meet the evening train the next day, we discovered our main source of entertainment — an overexuberant cocker spaniel puppy and a shy little two-year-old girl. What a place to spend your time in a national park! Both puppy and child belonged to the stationmaster and appeared to spend every day, all day long, playing on the station platform. Anne had great fun with both of them and four huge freight trains a day made the place even more exciting.

While the three little ones romped on their splintery wood playground, I had a chance to ask the stationmaster a little more about this farthest north railroad in North America (also the only government-owned one in the United States). In 1912 Congress passed an act setting up a commission to study the possibilities of a railroad in Alaska. On the basis of their findings, in 1915 Woodrow Wilson announced the selection of a route from Seward on the southern coast north 400 miles (through Anchorage) to the Tanana River area (where existing tracks continued to Fairbanks), with a branch line of thirty-eight miles to the Matanuska coal fields. The construction was completed in 1923, with a gold spike driven in by President Warren G. Harding. Today the railroad runs ultramodern streamliners daily in both directions between Fairbanks and Anchorage, the trip taking about twelve hours, and I heard that besides the reclining chairs and huge windows for sightseeing, they even stop the train at a certain point along the Susitna River on clear days so that the passengers can get out and take pictures of Mount McKinley.

One day we did join the tourists — taking a short bus ride down to park headquarters to watch the sled dogs being hitched to a sled (with wheels) for their daily exercise. Park rangers use the huskies there all winter because the road is closed by snow from September until June. The dogs were beautiful Malemutes, large and powerful, with thick fur coats and slant eyes. They seemed very used to people, friendly and lazy, until they were hitched to the sled and told to move — "Mush." They took off in a flash and pulled the park ranger down a trail in a great burst of speed. It took him twice around before he could calm them down enough to stop them. Then they suddenly became friendly and lazy again and let everybody pat them.

Another day we wandered a short way down one of the park's paths. The area had looked so bleak and desolate from the air that I wanted to get a closer look at just what really did grow in this subarctic region. All the trees and shrubs were carefully labeled so that any neophyte like me could tell at a glance, for instance, that the commonest tree in the park — a stunted, gnarled evergreen — was the white spruce. From the air we had seen spruce forests along the big rivers. Cottonwoods, aspen, willow (thirty different types!), and dwarf birch also grow along the rivers, but above these alluvial areas the trees give way abruptly to the vast stretches of tundra. According to the little park signs, there are two kinds of alpine tundra — shrubby plants of the "wet" variety at lower elevations and the matlike plants of the "dry" tundra covering the hills and lower mountain slopes. On closer inspection, lovely flowers brighten the harsh landscape.

Mountain azalea, forget-me-nots (the Alaska state flower), blue lupine, larkspur, and monkshood (a flower which Lowell encountered in Tibet) cover the meadows, but are half hidden by the tundra bushes so that we could not see them from the air. We did see the white, pink, and blue native pea flowers which often completely cover the gravel bars of the rivers.

The mosses and lichens are equally widespread and most important. The former helps conserve water and insulate the frozen soil from the warm summer sun, while the latter is an indispensable food for many of the animals.

And just what kind of animals are around us, I kept wondering as we wandered down the isolated path. I half-expected a bear or moose as we rounded each corner. But I learned later that the moose and grizzly bears are usually too shy to come that close to where so many people are living. The Alaska moose is the largest animal in the park, the bulls weighing nearly three fourths of a ton. They prefer living in the spruce forests, but often stand in the water of the lakes and ponds in the summer, we were told, to escape the heat and bugs. Their food comes almost entirely from the willow trees — twigs, bark, flowers, and leaves.

The Toklat grizzly bears roam all through the park, but prefer the open tundra. Mr. Bear will settle for both plant food and animals. They will spend hours stalking Dall sheep and caribou, or chasing mice, squirrels, and marmots, but will usually end up eating roots, grasses, and berries.

The grizzlies are a lighter color than the Alaska brown bear (which is really black!) and often bleach to a straw color under the summer sun. They grow new dark coats in the autumn and then retreat to the shelter of their winter dens in October. Babies (often twins) are born during the winter, and the mother takes care of them until they are two years old.

Then there are the Dall sheep and caribou, which we saw from the air (the European caribou are smaller and are actually the reindeer of Santa Claus fame), and the smaller animals include the snowshoe rabbit, lynx, coyote, fox, and an occasional wolf. All the animals must be well adjusted to the severe northern climate. Many of the countless insects have unusual ways of getting through the winter, and some of the animals and most birds simply depart for warmer latitudes. One pleasant fact for queasy women — no snakes or turtles in McKinley Park at any time of year!

Birds, I discovered when I went to a lecture on them at the hotel one night, are among the most fascinating inhabitants, and they are more "well traveled" than even their fellow Alaskan humans! The long-tailed jaeger spends each winter on islands on the far shores of the Pacific near Japan. The golden plover goes only as far as Hawaii, but the surf bird beats them all — some of them actually fly all the way south to the Strait of Magellan. For 150 years no one knew where these birds went to nest during the summer, and then one of their nests was discovered in McKinley Park in 1926. Apparently their homes are mostly in the mountains of the interior of Alaska, where man rarely goes.

Although we were in McKinley Park, we couldn't actually see its namesake, North America's highest mountain. If I had taken one of the tourist car rides (a gravel road goes about a hundred miles through the park from east to west, ending at the mining camp of Kantishna), I might have caught a few glimpses of "Denali," Indian name for "the high one." So, for all of us, the highlight of our visit to the park was our flight over the Alaska Range, virtually within reach of Mount McKinley. We had to return to Anchorage for a few days, and then our next stop was back to the park, to Camp Denali, the cluster of tents and cabins high on a ridge above Wonder Lake, near Kantishna, that ghost town which was the terminus of the park road. It was a spectacularly clear day — a deep cloudless blue sky, which is so unusual in the mountains during the summer months. So Lowell decided that rather than follow the railroad to the park hotel again, then the road west to the camp, we would go direct, crossing the mountains just east of McKinley itself. Leaving Talkeetna behind us, we turned northwest, climbing to 9000 feet, following one of McKinley's wide, curving glaciers. It was a ribbon of black at the bottom, but turned white up higher, crisscrossed by thousands of crevasses. I wondered where one could ever land a little plane there! Better not to think such thoughts, but concentrate on the view, which was spectacular: McKinley towered above us to our left, its steep sides pock-marked by snow and ice slides, its ice-covered rock ridges glistening in the sun. The area between us and the big mountain was a mass of jumbled rock and snow peaks, with glaciers in-between. The largest of these lie in the Yentna and Chulitna river basins, exposed to the moisture-laden winds of the Pacific.

We could see three other impressive peaks rising close to McKinley: Mount Foraker (17,395 feet), Mt. Hunter (14,573 feet), and Mt. Brooks (11,939 feet). Just before we reached the northern saddle, to the east of Brooks Peak, at the head of the big Muldrow Glacier, Lowell spotted three orange tents on the snow below. A climbing party! We circled and saw people standing around, waving. How amazing to chance upon such a little dot of humanity in the middle of such a vast wilderness! They were one of the many mountaineering groups who have tested their strength against the weather and steep icy slopes of this great mountain.

McKinley is actually crowned by two peaks. The true summit is the South Peak (20,320 feet), two miles from the

19,470-foot North Peak. The first successful ascent of the North Peak was made in 1910 by, ironically enough, two Alaskan sourdoughs, William Taylor and Pete Anderson. It wasn't until 1913 that a party led by Archdeacon Hudson Stuck and Harry Karstens reached the summit of the South Peak. In 1932 the Lindley-Liek group was the first to climb both peaks, and they were also the first to go all the way on skis, according to our Stowe, Vermont, friend Erling Strom, who was a member of that expedition.

Another of our friends received distinction on the mountain, but in a different way — she was the first woman to reach McKinley's summit. Barbara Washburn's husband, Brad, was leader of an expedition that tackled the mountain in 1947. When Barbara married Brad in 1941, she was a secretary from Englewood, New Jersey, and had never even been near the foot of a mountain. Brad took her to the Fairweather Range in southeastern Alaska on their honeymoon and introduced her to climbing by leading her to the top of Mount Bertha. Lowell can swear to that fact because he was with them, too! What a honeymoon, with five teen-age boys (along to help carry equipment) thrown in in the bargain!

Mentally, we, too, were climbing McKinley as we stared out the windows at the majestic mountain. *Charlie* was climbing slowly, so that we could slip over the final ridge to the north. Anne had long since gone to sleep, curled up on her comfortable back seat. Once above that ridge, the flat tundra terrain of the park stretched all about us — no foothills around McKinley here, just an almost sheer drop of over 17,000 feet. We descended rapidly now, following the great Muldrow Glacier, over 55 miles long and one of the main approaches to McKinley for climbers.

We knew the park road which went past Camp Denali to Kantishna skirted the glacier en route so that we had no trouble picking it up. The camp itself sits on a ridge just north of Wonder Lake, only two miles outside the park boundary. The lake is a famous landmark — a big oval, of beautiful sapphire blue. When standing on its shore, one sees McKinley just beyond, and a magnificent reflection of the mountain on the waters of the lake. A big old bull moose ("old faithful," local folks call him) makes his home near there and most obligingly stands in the shallow water each evening, adding the finishing touch to the perfect picture for anyone with a camera.

We buzzed low over the camp, a signal to come meet us, then flew on up a narrow canyon where we found the Kantishna airstrip. The people at the park hotel had told us the strip was unusable, but I talked to the camp owners about it when they came to meet a train, while Anne and I were "living" at the railroad station. They said that they were flying in and out of it all the time, that it was just a bit tricky for novice pilots.

Now, looking down on the strip beneath us, I knew what they meant — it looked like nothing but a rough gravel bar from the air, sandwiched in-between canyon walls. Lowell made a steep turn and dragged it — coming low over a stream at one end, heading for tall trees not too far ahead. "It's fine," he said, as I was wringing my hands in despair. Two more of the steepest turns, and we floated down over the water, hitting hard, bouncing roughly on the uneven stones and grass hummocks. We came to a stop quickly, which was just as well, what with the bushes looming up ahead. And Anne was still sound asleep in the back!

We got out to push the plane to one side and were greeted by a swarm of mosquitoes, our first real encounter with the Alaskan "giant bomber" variety. They especially liked Anne, and she didn't quite know how to stave them off. Fortunately the jeep from the camp arrived before things got too far out of hand. The driver was Jinny Wood — she and her husband, Woody, are co-owners with Celia Hunter, a former woman aviator during World War II. When Woody was a ranger in McKinley Park, he made the first traverse of McKinley and many other ascents in the area. The two women have hiked and camped in Europe and the mountains of our Far West, as well as Alaska.

It was while Jinny and Woody were hiking together in the Wonder Lake area that they fell in love with this particular hilltop location. It is one of the few spots outside of the park that has an unrestricted view of Mount McKinley. When he left the Forestry Service to study engineering, they built this camp to run as a small-scale tourist operation during the summers. We have since heard that business has boomed in the last two seasons and that Jinny and Woody have found themselves a full-time occupation, especially between May and October.

Their new tourist information brochure states:

> "*Camp Denali is not for everyone*. We feel our wilderness is rather special to be enjoyed by rather special people. We do not believe in 'giving the public what it wants,' but would rather find the people who are looking for the sorts of things Camp Denali and its majestic surroundings have to offer. We have designed our Camp to be subordinate to the natural surroundings, not to dominate them. We do not have electricity, modern plumbing or refrigeration. Neither do we have juke boxes, T.V., or a bar."

And that is the absolute truth, as we soon discovered for ourselves.

We had a three-mile drive through the canyon and up the hill, past the old ghost mining town of Kantishna. Once, during the height of the gold rush, 1200 people lived

there, but now we saw only a few deserted, crumbling
shacks. The last resident died the year before, Woody told
us, and happened to be a woman with a colorful personality
and an equally colorful past. She was Fanny Quigley, a dance-
hall girl who came to Kantishna from the Klondike in 1906.
She married Joe Quigley (he was over six feet four, she less
than five feet tall) and, between them, they had mines and
claims all over the area. Despite her size she could mush
dogs, hunt and trap, and also raised one of the best gardens
in Alaska. They say she could swear like a trooper, had a
terrible temper, and drank like a fish. But no one was ever
bigger-hearted or kinder to anyone in need of food or shelter.

In her later years (after Joe had left her) she built the
only frame house in Kantishna and was responsible for having the air strip built! Woe to any pilot who landed on a
sand bar nearer town instead of her runway. She would
meet him with an ax and tell him in no uncertain terms
that she had built that strip and meant to have it used.
She finally died just a few years ago — some say because
she quit drinking for three days!

Sticking out like a sore thumb among those ghost buildings was a brand-new trailer and a sign beside the creek to
our left: "Private property, no trespassing." Another prospector was at work, panning for gold. Someone found a two-
hundred-dollar gold nugget there last year, and that started
the search all over again. All the tourists that come to Camp
Denali are usually brought to Kantishna to try their hand
at panning. Most of them come away with tiny particles of
gold (they stick them to pieces of Scotch tape to keep them
from being lost), but the general belief now is that the
creek is "mined out." We were amazed at the number of
people we encountered all over Alaska who were still spending time and energy seriously expecting to "strike it rich"

by finding gold. We had thought that gold-panning prospectors were a colorful product of the past, but not so!

On to the camp, up a steep hill dotted with little tent cabins — canvas tops, with black stovepipes sticking out the tops, and wood floors. They were perched amid the tundra bushes, with little matchbox "petunias" out back and tiny log signs in front. Each had its own name — "Perma Frost," "Nugget," "Sub-Zero," and others. These were the quarters for the tourists with cars and housekeeping equipment. We passed a small "general store" (the smallest in existence, no doubt) where these people could get some canned goods. Then up at the top of the ridge we came to the more permanent part of the camp — four one-room log huts, a larger community dining-living room, and several other scattered cabins, for laundry, storage, a shower, and rooms for the folks working at the camp.

Anne was thrilled with our "very own house" and called it her home while we were there. We were given a cabin that was large enough for three bunk beds (with sleeping bags), a little wood stove, a table and two log benches, and some shelves. It was cozy and comfortable, and we loved every moment in it. We spent most of our time on its little front porch, enjoying the spectacular view of Mount McKinley. On the practical side, we had our own "petunia" just out back (I brought along Anne's airplane potty, though, to avoid trips with her in the middle of the night), and a small plastic hose with a spigot on the end brought cold stream water straight to our porch. Here we washed ourselves and our clothes and dishes (I cooked most of Anne's meals over our primus stove because camp dinner hours were late for her) — a total lack of privacy, but how much better than having to walk to the stream! We made a very pleasant discovery, too. When the sun was out, it heated up those plastic pipes so that by noon each sunny day we had hot water — really hot! Wonderful for showers, with bathing suit on, and I saved all my laundry and dishes to do then. (If we wanted a more complete shower, we collected soap and towel and headed up the hill past the eating cabin to a tiny hut containing a wood-burning hot-water heater, shower spigot, and perpetual clouds of steam.)

The day we arrived, the other three cabins near us were filled with older couples from the Anchorage and Fairbanks areas. So when J.P., Mike, Merrill, and Bill Bouchat (an Alaskan, a university student who joined us to perform all the odd jobs, of which there were many!) flew in from Fairbanks, they had to pitch tents in the tundra beside us. Once settled in, we all took a two-day holiday to just plain enjoy our surroundings. Beneath the shadow of Mount McKinley, we basked in the sun and went swimming. A little round pond shared the ridge with us, nestling in the tundra just below the dining hall. The water was clear and cold — too cold for me when I heard the bottom was in the permafrost! They assured me the top foot of water was well warmed by the sun, but that just didn't sound quite deep enough to me. However, the men had a great time swimming and splashing about and paddling little Eskimo kayaks. Mike is a good swimmer and every morning around eight, while we were having hot oatmeal cereal, wearing heavy sweaters against the early morning chill, looking out the dining-hall picture windows, we'd suddenly see Mike come dashing from his tent, take a running dive, and swim twice around the pond. Enough to chill the rest of us for the entire day. We called him our "icebreaker."

Mealtimes were most informal — everyone sitting on benches at two long tables, boardinghouse style. We had heavy mugs of steaming coffee or tea or cold powdered milk, muffins, pancakes, and pastries; tuna fish, crab meat, and ham casseroles, plenty of potatoes, and an occasional salad. Fresh vegetables were rare and meat was unheard of — partly because there was no refrigeration. No power — no lights, which one really didn't need since it never got dark anyway. Actually the sun did dip down behind the Alaska Range about ten at night, but to have it as bright as noon at 3 A.M. drove me to distraction. Once again, I spent my evenings devising ingenious ways to darken our room and thereby keep Anne asleep until 6 A.M. at the latest.

The camp had attracted an unusual assortment of helpers — the cook was a strong hefty gal who taught physical education at a small junior college during the winter. They called her Dolly. Her assistant was a small masculine woman who seldom said a word. She had an equally silent male friend named Rocky, and between meals they were always off panning for gold. A tall, thin, almost effeminate man appeared to be the dishwasher, and between meals he was always climbing mountains. A pretty blond college girl from Denver and a sweet, older gray-haired crippled woman completed the kitchen staff.

All was harmonious despite the great diversity in personalities, and everyone seemed to be there because they enjoyed the out-of-doors environment. Jinny and Woody virtually never have to look for someone to hire. Young men and women drift into camp and then decide (and are invited) to stay and take on some one particular job which needs to be filled at that particular moment. A college freshman from the West Coast came as a tourist one June, fell in love with the area, and took over the baking duties. When not in the kitchen, she was out collecting and pressing plants for her college herbarium. She transferred to the University of Alaska, returning to Camp Denali for two summers.

A Unitarian minister and his two children joined up for the summer, so that the younger ones could have a bit of outdoor life. He, a wizard with machinery, kept all equipment in top-flight shape during his stay there.

Two Australian girls who were working their way around the world arrived as guests in midsummer. They stayed on as needed kitchen hands and endeared themselves to everyone. But the camp was minus a cook last year, and they were forced to advertise in the normal manner. The advertisement did not ask for any normal sort of person, however, and Camp Denali finally went without a cook for the entire season.

> *Wanted*: a cook.
> The Camp Denali cook must be a unique person. She must be able to turn out tasty meals such as you would prepare if company were coming to dinner in your own home, rather than restaurant or institutional fare. She must be resourceful, imaginative, and economical, able to work without refrigeration, and electricity, and supplies that come in (save for limited fresh produce) with our one shipment of groceries. She must be able to take off her apron and sit down at the table as a gracious hostess, and she must have a congenial personality. . . . above all, she must like camp life and the surroundings, which are really the chief compensations for working at Camp Denali.

Anyone interested in applying next summer?

Equally happy, busy members of the camp were two little girls, one only a few months older than Anne and the other a little younger. Jeannie, the older, was the daughter of the gray-haired older woman and a very sweet well-behaved child. She and Anne became fast friends and played together all day long. She often came to our cabin to eat with Anne, and they read and crayoned together on the front porch.

It was wonderful for Anne, and me, too. I had more time to myself and could eat with the others, while Anne and Jeannie played just outside. The other little girl, Romany, the Woodses' daughter, was a little young for playing with them, but she usually tagged along and Anne enjoyed having someone to "mother." Their favorite "haunt" was the little plastic swimming pool just outside the dining hall. They splashed and played about in it by the hour — under the hot sun, with the snow-covered mountains just beyond. An incongruous picture which did not in the least concern the little ones.

Giving Anne a bath was quite a project. Jeannie's mother had two big laundry tubs, connected and sitting on a stand waist high. We filled them with warm water, put Anne in one and Jeannie in the other, and then the fun began.

One afternoon, while Lowell and the men were off working, the pretty blond college-student waitress asked me if I'd like to bring Anne and hike up to a little cabin on top of the hill behind us. She also asked Bill Bouchat to come along, and I felt that Anne and I were either to be chaperones or excess baggage. In any case, I was glad Bill was going along because I was not sure how far Anne would make it under her own steam, and I did not relish the idea of carrying her alone for any distance. (We had a little "pack chair" which Lowell used to carry her about on the icecap.) The hike would take about forty-five minutes, through the tundra and mud, and almost straight up the steep hill.

The reason for visiting the little cabin? A young couple and their eighteen-month-old boy lived there during the summer, while he engineered a big construction project in the park. I had met them at Camp Denali one day, the little boy in a rucksack on his daddy's back. They seemed a most attractive and interesting couple, and I was intrigued by

what their life might be like in such an isolated home.
We tramped up the narrow footpath, Anne stopping every
few moments to pick wild flowers or prance in the mud. Her
pace was slow, to say the least, and she had a miserable
time walking through the tundra bush, which came to her
shoulders. We finally decided, in view of the short time we
had, that we'd better take turns carrying her. I was glad I
had help.

We were all puffing and panting by the time we reached
the top, except Anne, who was singing and laughing, delighted with her joy ride. The little log house was perched
on top of a rocky outcropping, like an eagle's nest, we
thought, and that, we discovered later, was the cabin's name:
"Eagle's Nest." They had the same magnificent view of the
mountains, plus the isolation. The husband, Ted Lachelt,
was off getting water — the nearest source was a stream half
a mile away. But the wife, Barbara, and her little boy
seemed pleased to have some company. I doubt they ever
have many people just drop in, considering the climb.

The cabin was charming and homey. The front doorstep
and a little grassy area just beyond were encircled by a piece
of wire fencing, a safe place for the little boy to play. (Children that age could so easily get lost in the tundra.) Inside,
most of the one small room was a large double bed. Beneath it was a big "drawer" (with plenty of room between
it and the big bed for breathing space) which pulled out
to make a trundle bed! At night they put the little one to
bed early, closed the "drawer," so that he was in a dark,
quiet cubicle, and then had their dinner, read or enjoyed
music undisturbed. Shelves above the bed were jammed
with interesting-looking books, and a guitar hung on the
other wall, above a small sink. A Coleman stove, with a
small oven, stood against one wall, at the foot of the bed,

and the only other free corner had a small table and two log benches.

To complete the domestic picture, Barbara pulled open the oven door and brought out a batch of raisin cookies! We had to wait for something to drink until Ted came back from the stream, but he appeared soon, and we sipped cold glasses of Kool-Aid on the front doorstep. They told me that they spent each winter in a more civilized area, longing for the moment when they could return to the "Eagle's Nest," and that they hoped Ted could find enough engineering jobs in the area during the summers so that they could keep on living in their retreat. I heard later that they had to miss last summer because of a brand new baby girl and instead spent the warm months near an engineering job in more accessible Yellowstone Park. They will undoubtedly return to their "Eagle's Nest" next year, but where will they put their second trundle bed?

The men had been working hard those days, from early in the morning until late at night, thanks to the midnight sun. J.P. and Mike were filming the mountains in Merrill's plane, while Lowell spent each day in the air, scouting about for a possible site for a "survival" sequence. We needed a sand bar we could safely land on and camp out on. We could find nothing smooth enough, and finally he and Merrill went off together for a final try. The rest of us waited at camp, crossing our fingers. Around noon, Merrill's yellow Cessna roared over, circled, and came back even lower. I could see Lowell leaning out of the window, an object in his hand. They were dropping something, probably aiming for J. P. and Mike, who were standing by their tents. The only trouble was he let go too soon, and the white paper bag splashed into the pond. We all stood about, wondering what to do, hating to be the one to have to dive in on such a cold, cloudy day (there was always a swift change in climate the moment the sun disappeared), when Bill Bouchat appeared with one of the little kayaks. By now we were all laughing uproariously at the whole situation. The little white bag still bobbed up and down, and Merrill and Lowell were still circling anxiously overhead. We all placed bets as to what our little "treasure" might be. Ice cream, most of us thought, licking our chops.

Bill reached the missile in the nick of time and then infuriated all of us by just sitting in the boat, laughing at what he found. We finally got him to come in, discovered a cheap dime novel inside the bag (for ballast only) plus a penciled message: "Have no good bars, will have to move on this P.M." What an unhappy anticlimax!

I hated to leave such an attractive, comfortable spot so soon and Anne was distressed, but that was that — we'd have to pack up and fly off within a few hours, and I wondered where we could possibly find another beautiful, remote spot with a few of the comforts of modern living. I had visions of tents on a sand bar, swarms of mosquitoes, and cooking for five hungry men over a single primus stove.

Alaska—the forty-ninth state

Anchorage just after statehood was announced

Chilatna Lake: a "survival" scene

Camp Denali: Anne watches J.P. and Mike

Camp Denali: Anne and Jeannie enjoying their weekly bath

Porcupine Creek: Anne and Tay with the Stanish brothers

Tay and Anne outside Mr. and Mrs. Elijah Paniauk's house

CHAPTER X

On to Fairbanks, the Golden
Heart of the North

O UR next destination was a fishing camp, south of the Alaska Range on Chilatna Lake, complete with an airstrip right at the water's edge. Our flight across the mountains was another breath-taking adventure. The weather was crystal clear again, and this time we climbed to 10,000 feet, cutting across a 9000-foot ridge just to the right of Mount McKinley. It would have been much more prudent to fly higher over such rugged terrain, but we carried no oxygen. Also, we knew the air was smooth that morning, with little danger of downdrafts forcing us into the snow beneath. And at such a low altitude we felt like mountain climbers, enveloped in a silent, magnificent white world. Even my usual frightening forebodings were overcome by the thrill we both felt from such a sight. The mountain rose way above us just beyond our wingtip, and again we saw signs of climbers. A former camp site, on an icy plateau, and a trail of steps cut into the ice, leading upward, shining in the sunlight. At one point, on the steepest flank of the mountain, we suddenly saw a huge white cloud billow upward, then roll swiftly down the slope just beneath our wing — a dreaded avalanche!

We crossed a second ridge, then followed a glacier down the south side. Our map was a great help — the whole section was a big blank yellow! The only lettering in the middle of it said "unexplored." It's hard to believe that a part of the North American continent is still unmapped.

But fortunately that was no problem for us that day as we just followed the glacier on down, and lying at its foot was Chilatna Lake. I had not expected such a big one, with deep blue water. Sheer rock cliffs and the glacier enclosed three sides. The south shore was flat and sandy, and there we found the air strip, six or eight tents beside it, and a few small cabins at one end. The tents belonged to an oil company which had a group of geologists based there, busy looking for oil. And were they busy! They kept two helicopters and two big Grumman Gooses coming in and out all day and night. It was like living beside Idlewild Airport. The first night there both Gooses came in at 1 A.M., blasting us all out of bed, and left again at six o'clock. And the 'copters must have warmed up their engines at our front doorstep all night long.

But it was most convenient to park our own plane there and walk only a few steps to our cabin. We had a bigger one this time, with a large old wood stove for heat, a table and chairs, and a washstand for pitchers and pans. I missed our "running water." The main dining area was very similar to the other, but its front porch was just a few feet from the lake, with a lovely view of some of the smaller mountains behind. (McKinley itself was hidden.)

This camp is used for hunting and fishing parties, owned by one of the small Anchorage airlines and run by a hard-working young couple. In fact, I have never seen a woman work harder in my life. The day we arrived she was doing mountains of laundry in an old-fashioned washing machine, while a great stack of dirty dishes awaited her at the kitchen sink. (Equipped with an old-fashioned hand pump, which fascinated Anne — to think that water could come out of something so much more interesting than a faucet!) At this point, her washing machine broke down and she had to resort to big tin tubs and a plunger. The crowning blow came when she hung up a batch of clean sheets. Just then one of those infernal Gooses started its engines and blew dirt over the entire load! When Peggy just calmly took them down and washed them all over again, I vowed I would always remember her problems and patience when I tackled my housework.

And what delicious dinners she served us — steaks, roasts, veal cutlets, ice cream, and fresh milk. She had a giant freezer that was stocked with everything we could think of, run by a small generator. (We even had electric lights.) And best of all, she helped me prepare good meals for Anne at twelve and five-thirty, before others were ready to eat. This was a great help because Anne and I had lots of "acting" to do in the filmed survival sequence.

Charlie was pushed onto a tiny bit of sand, one wheel practically in the water, precariously atilt, his cowling off. This was his position for the next five days, and any number of worried airmen came rushing into the lodge to ask what had happened. But the purpose of the sequence was not what happened to the plane, but how we camped out: cooking, washing, fishing, and so forth. Unfortunately, most of it had to be done in a pouring rain.

For about two hours on Monday afternoon, when we first arrived, we had a little sunlight, and we filmed Anne fishing with her daddy and helping me do laundry (a big help that was), having dinner and going to bed. It was fun, especially since we didn't have to record any sound. I washed some clothes in the cold lake water and hung them up on *Charlie's* aerial to dry. Anne threw one of Lowell's socks out into the deeper water (without being told) and I had to wade out to retrieve it — good for the picture but bad for discipline. This time Anne willingly put on her pajamas, ate supper, and went to bed, but it began to rain before we were through. Fortunately, the rest of the pictures were of me cooking inside the tent, so Anne went back to the cabin with Daddy, while poor J.P. and Mike got soaked standing in the downpour outside the tent door, a tarpaulin over all of the camera but the lens.

Our family movie making came to a temporary halt the next morning when we hastily had to "evacuate" Anne to the nearest doctor. She had had three nosebleeds in four days (the first at Camp Denali), and it worried me considerably. I wasn't sure how to stop them, or what caused them. Then Monday night she was awake half the night complaining of a stomachache and Tuesday morning awoke with a fever. That settled it for me — at home I'd wait and see what might develop, but out here in the wilds, miles from any medical help, with bad weather threatening to turn worse and ground the plane, I just didn't want to take a chance. Lowell was planning to fly to Anchorage with Merrill anyway to pick up film supplies, so within the space of a few moments I packed a bag, bundled Anne up, and joined them in the plane.

We had a forty-five-minute flight under overcast skies, and, once at the Anchorage airport, I called a woman whose name I had been given by friends in Juneau. She was most friendly and gave me the name of her pediatrician. He was most unfriendly and said no more new patients, thank you. I certainly understood — one of the hazards of traveling. I tried several other doctors whose names I had been given, and one finally said to come right in.

Anne was protesting all the way and really kicked up a fuss when we saw the doctor. He suggested I leave the room (a normal procedure for some doctors, I gather — we weren't used to it because it wasn't the practice in our home town), which sent her into hysterics, and me, too. She finally did calm down and was sucking a lollipop when they returned. He was brief and brusque — merely said she had a nose infection, with a good deal of pus and quite a sore throat (the stomachache Anne complained about). He agreed we should stay in town a few days, wrote out a prescription (with no explanation), and that was that. It wasn't until we got back to the hotel that I learned from Anne, verified by the mark on her backside, that he had also given her a shot. I could only assume it was penicillin. It's a good thing she was not allergic to it.

I was feeling very homesick and alone at the hotel that night (Lowell and Merrill returned to the lake in the afternoon), but the next morning Anne was completely herself again. So we both looked forward to returning to Chilatna first thing the following day. That night I had another experience that unnerved me all over again. It was around nine o'clock — Anne had gone to sleep and I was sitting next to the window, reading by the light of the "midnight sun." All of a sudden the whole room seemed to be swaying. I closed my eyes in disbelief, but could feel it. I felt sick to my stomach and terrified! My first thought was "earthquake," but then I dismissed that — "not here, and out of the blue." Maybe it was a result of the wind blowing the Venetian blinds so close to my eyes. I got up and walked to the center of the room. There was still an obvious swaying motion there! I just gave up — "I'm worn out," I thought, and crawled right into bed. The next morning I never gave a thought to this incident until we arrived back at Chilatna Lake. Mike greeted me with, "Did you feel the earthquake last night at nine o'clock?" I have never felt such a sense of relief! Peggy also told me that she thought she was having a dizzy spell, until she looked around the kitchen and saw the pots, pans, and ladles all swinging back and forth.

Two days later we read newspaper accounts of the quake. It was a massive one, the strongest in Alaska in over sixty years, with a magnitude of eight on seismographs. (Earthquakes of that size occur anywhere only once or twice a year.) Lituya Bay, a virtually landlocked harbor near the Fairweather Range of southeast Alaska, was the center of the quake — fortunately, a wild, isolated area with no human habitation. Otherwise, many lives might have been lost. The bay is often used as a shelter by fishermen and has a long history of catastrophes, partly because of the extremely tricky entrance from the ocean and also because it does lie directly on the Fairweather Fault.

Three fishing boats were anchored in the bay that night — two disappeared from sight, although the occupants of one were eventually rescued, and the third came through unscathed, the father and son bringing back an incredible eyewitness account of the havoc wrought before their eyes. Great 10- and 15,000-foot mountains heaved and twisted, spewing up billowing clouds of snow and rock and starting tremendous rock avalanches. Large glaciers broke up, like little ice cubes being crushed, and threw tons of debris and ice into the bay. These millions of tons of ice, aided by the

earth's shock, started a huge wave which stripped the walls
of the bay to bedrock as high as 200 feet above the normal
water line. The speed of the wave was such that it stripped
the bark off all the trees it carried away. The survivors also
talked of a series of giant waves that raced back and forth
in the enclosed bay, the waters filled with tumbling icebergs,
trees, and other debris. The three little boats were carried
back out over the spit and dumped into the ocean. Two
immediately sank, but the third, by some miracle, stayed
afloat. I wonder if fishermen still seek out Lituya Bay as a
quiet, safe retreat?

I cannot skip over our flight from Anchorage back to
Chilatna Bay that day, a never-to-be-forgotten one for me.
Anne and I woke up early Thursday morning to find dismal,
rainy weather. We were supposed to be at the airport at
8 A.M., ready to leave with Merrill, who was coming in from
camp just to pick us up. When we got to the field (I was sure
he would not be able to come), the clouds were low, it was
pouring, and there was Merrill, waiting for us. He said that
it was clear about twenty miles out, so I got in without protest, but what a twenty miles! We flew along just above
the trees for a while, in the pouring rain. Then fog crept in
below us, and I timidly suggested I was all for turning back.
But Merrill assured me it was temporary, that he'd flown
in over fog and beneath clouds for a while — so that's
just what we did. The only comforting thought I had —
aside from the fact that I was with one of the best pilots
in the country today — was that we were over a broad flat
river valley. Then, when I had had just about enough, the
fog disappeared the clouds began to break up, and the
rest of the ride was most enjoyable, especially because we
saw many animals. We zoomed right over one big black
bear sauntering in a meadow. His coat was a glistening

jet black. He reared up when he saw us, then bounded off into the woods. On a sand bar nearby a mama moose was giving her two babies a drink of water — twins are a rarity among moose. In a meadow just beyond, two black bear cubs were rolling about, red tongues hanging out. We never did spot their mother. And just before we came to the air strip, we spotted two huge bull moose sitting side by side, chewing their cud. I've never seen such tremendous antlers. The airplane didn't bother them a bit, for they never moved a muscle. You doubt we could see so much detail from an airplane in the air? We did, believe me, because we were not over fifty feet high!

A few more days at Lake Chilatna, and then on north we flew, this time circling around the mountains because of the low clouds and light rain showers. We buzzed low over the McKinley Park Hotel, then followed the railroad on north to Fairbanks. I was glad to be leaving the mountains for the flat Tanana River valley because of the poor visibility, due largely to thick smoke and forest fires. But the mountains didn't seem to want to let us go without one last salute — just as we were coming out of the final low pass, we hit the biggest bump that either of us can ever remember. It was a lulu and came at a time when the air was relatively smooth. Lowell and I both hit the ceiling hard (his head put a big dent in the sun visor) and Anne rose several feet off the rear seat. A number of small articles flew off the back shelf, much to Anne's great surprise, but, otherwise, no harm was done. Some sudden change of air currents between the coast and the interior was the cause, I guess.

We first saw Fairbanks a good fifty miles away (we happened to be out of the smoke at that time), at the foot of more mountains — a wide flat plain between us, and forest fires scattered everywhere. What a shame to lose so much timber that way. The airfield was a tremendous one, the 9000-foot runway used by Pan American Boeings (later enlarged for airline jets), and there were plenty of signs of Wien Alaska Airline activity — a huge hangar, and yellow and silver DC–3s and C–46s everywhere. We parked by their hangar, and Merrill's brother, Dick (who is also a pilot for his dad's airline), drove us to town.

Fairbanks is often referred to as the Golden Heart of Alaska. One reason is that it is an unusually warm and friendly city. Also, it is considered home to more pioneers of the gold-rush era than any other part of Alaska. Not only was Fairbanks a booming gold town in its own right but it was also the base of supplies for many other strikes, including the Klondike area. Nor was their gold a short-lived bonanza as in so many other communities of that day. As recently as twenty years ago the Fairbanks population was 2500, and most of them were dependent upon gold for their livelihood.

The original prospector was not a man named Fairbanks — this second largest city in Alaska is named after a Charles Fairbanks, senator from Indiana under the McKinley administration! But the seemingly "far-removed" namesake was one of the few congressmen of that era who foresaw the possibilities of Alaska and did so much to help the territory's early development.

In 1902 a Captain Barnette docked his stern wheeler along the banks of the Chena, near the present site of Fairbanks, and started a small trading post, a base of supply for prospectors in the surrounding area. That same summer Felix Pedro struck gold in a Fairbanks creek, and men began stampeding from Dawson and the Klondike to get in on the diggings. At first it was thought that the finds were not of great value, but it was then discovered that most of the gold there was down deep in the frozen gravel. New mining machinery was brought in and by 1905 the yearly output reached $6,000,000. (Gold ore there was worth ten to fifteen dollars a ton, while in Juneau it was worth only a dollar a ton.)

The gold output continued to soar as other diggings were started, and Fairbanks became a rip-roaring boom town. An eighty-five-year-old local sourdough told the town newspaper last year that Fairbanks was wilder than Dawson in the early days. "In those days the saloons did not have any keys. They just stayed open." He said there were thirty-three bars on the main street, four blocks long, and they all had plenty of business! "The old Floradora Dance Hall did a booming business," he recalled, and several fortunes were made in it. One owner piled up $50,000 and headed for the states." And, the old-timer added, the alley outside the dance hall was lined with ten to twelve baby cribs on either side. Then he agreed that Fairbanks had certainly grown a lot quieter since then.

With World War II, the military arrived (it cost our government over $50,000,000 to build Ladd and Eielson Air Force Bases, both close to town). So now Fairbanks' biggest payroll is the military, and it has grown ten times in size in these last twenty years (53,000 area population). Gold mining is still a principal part of the economy (total Alaska gold output is now only $9,000,000 a year compared to $26,000,000 in 1940), the gold taken from creeks by the world's largest dredges and draglines. They say there's plenty of gold still there, but the cost of getting it out isn't really worth it.

We found Fairbanks a smaller, less bustling city than Anchorage. It's more like one of our unhurried but lively western towns, with one main street, plus many reminders of the old gold-rush days. Log cabins still stand among the modern stores and apartment houses. Bearded old prospectors still amble down the narrow paved streets, and there still seem to be a good many more bars than average. Deluxe movie theaters have replaced the colorful old dance halls of the past.

The hotel situation, we quickly discovered, was tough. On the spur of the moment (we seldom made reservations in advance), we were able to find rooms in the one hotel for only that night. And no dining room was an added blow. Fortunately we were right on the main street and there was a little jukebox diner just down the way.

The next day, just when we thought we would have to pitch our tents in a field, we found rooms in a new motel — the Travelers Inn — swank and ultramodern, the latest in stateside motels — a town of contrasts! Later we heard the fabulous life story of the man who built this motel, Walter Hickel. He arrived in Anchorage in 1940 with thirty-seven cents in his pocket. The oldest son of ten children of a German tenant farmer in Kansas, he took the first job that came his way. It happened to be a professional-boxing fight, and he had never boxed professionally before. But he won, and that started him on his way. He began building housing units in Anchorage: first four duplexes, then forty, and finally ninety housing units. Then he embarked on his luxurious motel idea — beginning in Anchorage. It was such a sensational success that Fairbanks citizens asked him to build one there. He did, and on an even larger and more deluxe scale. We readily agree that it is truly a modern Alaskan landmark.

Since 1957 Wally Hickel has built over ninety large Anchorage homes and has announced plans for a downtown twelve-story office building and twelve-story hotel. A Kansas farm boy has become a vital force in Alaska, a leader in business and civic affairs, a millionaire, and the father of five sons. He is a visionary who looks to the future, thinks Alaska is in for a period of tremendous growth, and it sounds like he will undoubtedly be one of those leading the way.

We spent a good deal of our time in Fairbanks, walking up and down the streets, just looking or shopping for one thing or another. Two goings on which remain outstanding memories: the extremely active newsboys and the extremely active F–102 jets. It seemed one bombarded us from the ground and the other from the air all day long. We gathered that the local newspaper, the Fairbanks *News-Miner*, was a progressive one, especially when it came to sales campaigns among the newsboys. Endless streams of them walked up and down the streets all day long, calling "Buy paper." (Back home, months later, Anne convulsed us by suddenly calling, "Buy paper!")

The jets came from huge Eielson Air Force Base, an ever-busy SAC installation. When we weren't dodging newsboys, our eyes were on the sky, watching the formations of maneuvering planes.

One afternoon we saw an exciting film in the local movie theater — some of our own pictures. The home office sent out samples of our work thus far, and we had a great time taking a look at it. I was interested in seeing what Anne's reaction would be — she sat as if hypnotized at first, then began asking, "What's Anne doing?" Very soon she had had enough and spent the rest of the time happily exploring the darkened theater.

In our wanderings about town we came upon one of the major tourist attractions, the only stern-wheel excursion river boat in Alaska. Captain Jim Binkley steers it (his father was a famed Yukon River captain) and takes visitors up and down the Tanana River all summer, stopping to visit Indian fishing camps and sourdoughs. In the early days Fairbanks was a terminus for river boats bringing freight up from the ocean (via the Yukon River). The town relied on the stern-wheelers for most of its food supplies and mail. It was always a big occasion when the first boat came in following the spring breakup.

This breakup is a popular event in Fairbanks. A half-million dollar lottery is based on the exact time that the ice on the Tanana River breaks up. A favorite winter event is the annual fifty-mile championship dog-sled races. Oddly enough, the winters the past few years have been so mild that snow has been brought in from farther north to cover bare spots along the course!

Mild is hardly the word for Fairbanks winters, though, or summers either. Inland, and hemmed in by the mountains, the climate is pleasantly dry, but is one of great temperature extremes. Winters are cold (minus ten to minus sixty-six degrees), while summer temperatures range from sixty to ninety degrees, often around eighty.

One such hot day, when we were able to borrow a car, we drove a few miles northwest of Fairbanks to the town of College, home of the fast-growing, liberal arts University of Alaska. On the way, we passed through the farmland of the Tanana Valley (smaller than Matanuska in area), a rich soil area which is developing fast, despite the rigors of hard winters and permafrost. The long hours of summer sun make the crops mature even faster than along the coast. And for some reason (maybe the midnight sun!), calf production is ninety per cent or better up there. Dairy farming is the most prevalent occupation at the moment, and the big barns, cows, and broad green fields made us feel right back home in New Jersey.

The university's campus so typifies Alaska! The buildings are all modern, of strong simple design, and stand on a bare wind-swept hilltop, with thick green pines beneath and a magnificent view of the plains and hills almost encircling it. There was busy construction work going on everywhere — rapidly expanding from a few buildings to a sprawling campus. Nine hundred students studied there in the fall of '58, and a total of 1000 is expected within the next year or so. Dr. Ernest Patty, the university's president, hopes to keep the student body at that size, with the ratio of eight students to one teacher, and maintain emphasis on the quality of education rather than size. Dr. Patty stated that they wished to put "greater stress on making the institution a prestige university with a distinguished faculty and to capitalize on its Far North environment." A prime example is their internationally known Geophysical Institute, a center of research studies of the polar and subarctic regions.

In addition, Dr. Patty plans to introduce Russian language courses and worked for an exchange program between students of his university and Russian students. The president is a far-seeing man and also states, "We think the North Polar Basin is going to become one of the great research centers with its extensive land masses fringing the polar basin ocean and floating ice fields. The shortest distance between San Francisco and Bombay is through Fairbanks — the route of the future once we get agreements with Russia for refueling stops in that country."

The highlight of our Fairbanks stay for us was our visit with the Wiens, Merrill's mother and father. We had heard a great deal about both of them — he is one of Alaska's foremost pioneer bush pilots, the first to fly across the Arctic Circle. Noel learned to fly back home in Minnesota in 1921 and joined a flying stunt circus for a while. He went to Fairbanks in 1924 to fly for Jimmy Rodebaugh, ferrying up a new plane in the process. His flight from Anchorage to Fairbanks was the first between Alaska's two major cities.

He followed the railroad all the way, but at one point his wheels were practically rolling on the tracks because he could barely see through the thick smoke of forest fires. He finally reached Fairbanks, delivered the plane, and shook hands with his new employer. He told Rodebaugh he had hugged the track most of the way. "What did you do when you came to the sixty-foot overhead bridge at Dead Man's Slough?" "What bridge?" was the reply. Noel thinks he must have flown right under it.

Noel persuaded his three brothers to come up and join him during the twenties. Ralph became a crack pilot, but was killed in an experimental plane at Kotzebue in 1930. Brother Fritz was one of the ablest mechanics in Fairbanks, became vice-president in charge of operations. Brother Sig became a bush pilot, too, and is now president of the enterprise. The four brothers started Wien Alaska Airlines in 1927, buying one of Rodebaugh's old standards — Alaska's first scheduled airline and still the only line connecting the cities of the Alaskan North, and with extensive bush-pilot operations all over the Arctic. The thought of flying scheduled operations there in mid-winter amazes me. Their favorite publicity picture is of a Wien Alaska plane on the snow, with a sled-dog team beside it.

Mrs. Wein is quite a person in her own right. She is a strong, handsome, dark-haired woman, with a soft-spoken but sure manner. She played a role in the fight for statehood and then ran (but was defeated) for the State Senate last year. All I could think of, when first meeting her, was that she must have nerves of steel to have lasted through some of her husband's hair-raising flying episodes! Just listening to Noel recount stories of their early bush-pilot days was a fascinating and frightening experience for me. Noel was known as a cautious pilot, a man who carefully calculated his risks first. Even so, many early flights ended with a long walk out — not just a day's jaunt, but one- and two-week hikes, in mid-winter, too.

In 1925 Noel became the first man to fly over the Arctic Circle, in an open-cockpit Hisso Standard (old army training plane). He carried two prospectors from Fairbanks to Wiseman (in the Brooks Range), and on his return trip he encountered heavy winds which were blowing harder than his airplane could fly — sixty miles an hour. He finally ran out of gas just going nowhere and had to sit down on a sand bar forty air miles from Fairbanks. He had to walk overland for three days, in water up to his knees from the spring runoff, and with only two stale buns for food. "I made sure," he said, "that I would never go out unprepared again." That same year he had to crash-land on top of a hill near Livengood, and he and two passengers hiked out twenty-two miles along the winter dog-team trail to Fairbanks. He considered that a mere "Sunday jaunt."

Shortly after that episode, Noel made the first commercial flight to Nome in a five-place Fokker, but he landed at that town three days before his passengers did. A feat which requires explanation! He had to make a forced landing, due to bad weather, and while his pessimistic passengers chartered a boat from a nearby town for the rest of their journey, Noel stayed with the damaged plane, was able to repair it and fly it out to complete the trip.

Noel says a lot of his airline's early success is partly due to the strong old Stinson Detroiter, a plane built in 1926. He loves to tell another story, demonstrating its ruggedness. He was flying back to Fairbanks from McGrath just before Christmas in 1927, hurrying in order to take Christmas mail to Nome the next day. About halfway there, darkness descended, and he decided to spend the night at Lake Minchumina, at a small roadhouse there. He parked the plane in deep snow at the edge of the lake, then went into the inn for some roast moose meat. A wind came up, and when it grew stronger, he decided to go out and tie the airplane down. He found all the snow blown off the lake, and the Stinson, too! It had been blown out of sight, completely across the lake. He found it virtually impossible to walk on the glassy ice in the forty-mile wind, so gave up until the next morning. With daylight, he found the Stinson about a mile out on the lake, sitting upright and virtually undamaged. The right wing was stuck in drifted snow, though, and when he walked back to get a shovel, the wind came up again, blew the snow and the plane away again. Noel spent the next two days inside (one was Christmas), a northeaster howling around the cabin. The wind finally died down, and the plane was found in the brush on the far side of the lake, deep in snow, but intact. Noel flew it right out, and the Nome Christmas mail arrived over New Year's. A sturdy plane all right!

I thought Noel's most exciting story was the one about the Fox film expedition. They chartered two planes from Wien Alaska Airlines to fly up to the Arctic coast and film Eskimo polar bear and whale hunts. Noel had to hire another plane and pilot to help out (his was a one-man operation at that point), and picked a fellow bush pilot, Russell Merrill. A radio call north to Wiseman (a mining camp at the foot of the Brooks Range) confirmed good weather that far. But beyond lay the uncharted Brooks Mountains and the unexplored Arctic slopes north to Barrow. There was no way of knowing what the weather would be up there, so that the two heavily loaded planes took off on the morning of May 13, hoping to land in Barrow that evening and then return the next day. They did not return, and no word was heard from them for the next three and a half weeks! As Mrs. Wien said, "There was absolutely nothing to do but wait, hope, and pray."

After leaving Wiseman, Noel told us, the two planes climbed up to 2000 feet to clear the mountains. They crossed the range in perfect weather, then headed for the Colville River, which would take them toward Barrow. Their maps were a total blank now, and they navigated partly by compass, but mainly by pilot direction. Then they ran into a fog bank, with no hope of finding Barrow and not enough gas to return to Wiseman. They decided to land on one of the hundreds of lakes, got down safely, and then all crawled into sleeping bags. The next morning was clear, and Noel took off for Barrow, leaving his load behind with Merrill — his plan being to bring back fuel for the remaining plane. He reached Barrow and then quickly returned, but now he really had problems. There were thousands of similar lakes beneath him, and no landmarks whatsoever. He spent days alternately searching or, on the ground at Barrow, waiting out the fog. Once he, too, spent five days on a lake waiting out a snowstorm. He finally found Merrill's plane, but no men. Merrill's log, left in the plane, stated that the two cameraman passengers had started to walk north toward Barrow, and finally he, too, set out on foot, heading for the river and then along that to the coast. Noel and a fellow bush pilot, Matt Nieminen, kept on searching, and the latter finally spotted two men walking along the beach about fifty miles from Barrow. It was the cameramen, and they were just about to collapse, after eleven days of walking in crusted snow, their toes frozen and faces swollen and black. Their only food had been rice, and both men lost forty pounds. It is a miracle that they survived at all.

Merrill was found a day later by a trader with a dog team,

in almost the same spot. He had to spend some time in hospitals at Barrow and Nome and finally arrived back home three months later. It was a rugged ordeal for many people, but much was learned about Arctic flying, its weather, and the dos and don'ts required of the new technique. (And that's where our friend Merrill Wien got his first name!) The stories could go on and on, each equally as thrilling and hair-raising as the next. And the saga of bush flying contains the names of many others: Joe Crossen, Ben Eielson, Harold Gillam, Bob Reeve, and so on, who made equally thrilling and great contributions to the growth of aviation in Alaska.

Today seven Wiens are helping run the airline, employing another fifty pilots who fly a large number of big passenger planes. Their safety record is tops, and Noel, always the cautious one, has imbued one and all on the number-one importance of safety in the air. Now, thanks to modern equipment, radio aids, and techniques learned the hard way, passengers never have to "walk back."

But the bush pilots still carry on with much of the daring and excitement of old. They still fly single-engine airplanes, covering a vast empty region. They are still the vital life line for the many Eskimos, trappers, and prospectors scattered all over the north. They carry in mail and supplies and carry out messages, sick people, or expectant mothers, and perform countless little errands and services which mean so much to an isolated person. Fortunately for Alaska, and for all of America, they are carrying on the traditions of courage and daring, the selfless service to others which the bush pilots of the past pioneered.

CHAPTER XI

North of the Arctic Circle

Time to move on again — back to the airport early on the morning of the fifteenth for another historic flight of sorts for us — *Charlie* would cross the Arctic Circle for the first time that day. Lowell taxied the plane up to the hangar from the tie-down area to load up. When I lugged some of our countless little bundles over toward him, I noticed a look of great consternation on his face. He was bending over the tail wheel and, from the looks on the faces of the two mechanics, too, I realized something was definitely wrong. More endless waiting at an airfield! The tail-wheel tire rim had developed a large crack, and while it was not overly serious, it was nothing to fool around with, what with all the rough landings and take-offs which lay ahead. It was the rough landing areas, with loose stones and so forth, which had undoubtedly caused the crack in the first place.

So time out for several hours while the Wien mechanics gave *Charlie* a new tail-wheel tire. We were lucky to be at a big airfield, with expert help and airplane parts available.

I did not worry about having to entertain Anne — she was content, as usual, to wonder about the hangar, looking at the planes, visiting with the mechanics, and collecting the usual offerings of chewing gum and Coca-Cola. I did take her over to the cafeteria in the airport terminal, though, for a substantial lunch, as we had a long day ahead of us. The terminal was big and modern, a busy, bustling scene which impressed and, in a way, amazed me. Exactly like scenes at any of the big city airports in other states — Alaskans, the inveterate travelers, and a constant stream of visitors and tourists.

With *Charlie* in shape again, we took off around 2 P.M. for the two-hour flight due north to Bettles, a small CAA station at the foot of the Brooks Range. Merrill was just ahead of us and a Wien DC–3 just behind, also bound for Bettles. The weather was cloudy, with scattered showers, so we had to stay low — and how we bumped! The country was all hilly, so the up- and downdrafts were brutal. Anne curled up and went right to sleep, but I was feeling tired and squeamish and worried. Just north of Fairbanks, a huge forest fire covered miles along our route with thick layers of smoke. It was almost like entering the clouds, with visibility down to a mile for ten or fifteen minutes at a time. I didn't worry so much about getting lost, or about the hills around us. It was the thought of that DC–3 just behind that was driving me to distraction. Lowell told me to stop being so silly, then tried calling its captain over our radio. No luck, which didn't help matters a bit. Wien Fairbanks then came in over the earphones and said that the DC–3 had climbed above the clouds at 6000 feet, but was now forced to come back down. The lady radio operator added in a relaxed, cheery voice: "We'll radio him your position." Great! How I worried and searched for a glimpse of that plane during our entire flight, only to discover when we reached Bettles that he had wandered off course and was then many miles to the west and a good fifteen minutes behind us.

We could understand how easily one could wander there. We saw almost no landmarks beneath us during the entire flight — just hills covered with tundra. No roads (except a dirt one to Livengood, just north of Fairbanks, the farthest north road on our continent), virtually no rivers or open fields. I couldn't think of a more horrible spot for a forced landing. We flew on a compass heading, which we carefully checked when we reached the Yukon River, our halfway mark and a welcome sight. We were thrilled to see "the mighty Yukon" we had always heard so much about, but I think I was even more thrilled to see those long flat sand bars, perfect landing areas in an emergency. The river itself was much broader than we had expected. It was like flying over the Mississippi.

Soon afterward we could see higher mountains up ahead and knew Bettles was just before them. The Eskimo town of Bettles was a clump of wood huts on the Koyukuk River at the foot of the Brooks Range, but we were headed for the nearby long, gravel air strip, with eight or ten wooden buildings scattered along its edge.

Mike and J.P. greeted us after we landed with, "Boy, what a time Merrill gave us when we crossed the circle." We had been so busy worrying about our location and other silly things that we had completely forgotten that imaginary line! I decided it was just as well when I heard their story. They had been deeply engrossed in their books, their minds miles away, when the plane suddenly went into a sickening dive. They both thought it was the end, until they saw the grin on Merrill's face. He leveled off, told them they had been "duly initiated," and the chilly atmosphere gradually returned to normal. How Lowell would have loved to pull something like that on me!

It was now almost five in the afternoon, Anne was hungry again, and I was wondering where we were to stay. I knew there was no hotel there, and Lowell and Merrill had been extremely vague about accommodations. I had heard talk about the possibility of tents, but was hopeful that we would at least find a room (even a storeroom) for Anne. It would be much cooler here, and Anne and a sleeping bag still weren't reconciled. Also, a tent could not keep out that infernal midnight sun. Besides, I had become accustomed to some sort of accommodations always turning up, so I had not really given the lack of a hotel at Bettles a thought.

Until that moment, that is. The men looked worried, discussing it among themselves, while Anne and I sat on a bag, wondering what would happen next. A large sign by the tie-down area welcomed us to Bettles, told us we were five degrees above the Arctic Circle, that the local population was thirty-five, and that the temperature could go to sixty below zero. Just below this encouraging message of welcome, a wooden boardwalk led to a two-story log house. It was owned by Wien Airlines as a sort of guest house for any passengers unlucky enough to be stranded in that wilderness overnight. The airlines in Fairbanks had told us that all the rooms were taken at present by construction workers building a school for the CAA families, and a group of army engineers on a survey mission. Merrill surveyed the situation after landing and told us that the men could spread out their sleeping bags in an upstairs recreation room, and that Anne and I could use the bedroom of the Wien representative there for one night anyway. The Wien man was Jim Anderson (Andy), a blond Swede who flew bush operations for Wien in this area and ran their Bettles operation. His wife and two children had gone to Fairbanks for a brief visit and were not expected until the following day. He would move into his little girl's room and we could use the big double bed in his room. Sharing a bed with wiggly Anne, who threw herself all over her own bed all night long, was a horrible thought, but better than a tent.

So we trooped up to the guest house and, while the men went upstairs, we were taken through the kitchen to a tiny room out back. It had lovely curtains and bedspread, a handsome rug, and matching modern furniture. A little bit of home way up there. I noticed a picture of a pretty Eskimo woman and two children on Anne's bureau, and felt sudden surprise. I quickly remembered, though, that this was all a natural part of Alaska and began looking forward to meeting and becoming acquainted with Mrs. Anderson. The only trouble was, upon her return, we would lose our bed. Anne was enjoying Christmas in July: the children's bedroom next to ours and the attractive little sitting room between us and the kitchen were filled with toys. Meanwhile, I investigated food possibilities. A young Eskimo girl was bustling distractedly between sink and stove, and I gathered from a few mumbled words that all the construction gang and army mission ate at five-thirty at the long table in the big entrance room. I also gathered that there weren't any seats left for any of us and that the poor girl was at a complete loss as to what to do next. Andy appeared just then, suggesting two shifts, our group eating later, and told me to help myself to the cellar storeroom and kitchen in order to feed Anne. What a great help! And how nice to be on my own in a kitchen again. I explored the well-stocked storeroom, found plenty of soup, spaghetti, rice, and powdered milk, but little meat and no fresh vegetables there. The last thing to concern a two-year-old, and she wolfed down rice and vegetable soup for supper and went to bed, clutching her bottle filled with powdered milk.

I crawled in very shortly afterward, hoping Anne would spend the night well over on her side of the small bed. But oh no, she was so delighted to find me next to her that she showered me with hugs and kisses, then snuggled up as close as she could get. I kept shoving her back and she kept snuggling closer until I found myself teetering on the edge of the bed. I thought things would improve when she fell asleep, but after any number of sharp kicks in my head and stomach while my little one rolled all over the bed in her sleep, I finally gave up and retreated to the floor on a blanket.

The next morning began busy days of housekeeping for me. If we were to have a roof over our heads, I had to help cook and serve meals for our group of seven, wash dishes, do all their laundry in an antiquated machine in the cellar, and iron what seemed to be mountains of shirts and pants. One advantage to housekeeping in the Far North — I could hang out laundry after supper and it would be dry the next morning, thanks to the midnight sun. But, despite the hard work, I thoroughly enjoyed it. It had been so long since I'd been a housewife. Besides, I enjoyed the company of the young Eskimo girl, and of Hannah Anderson, who came back the next day. Hannah was a lovely young woman, probably in her early thirties, friendly, efficient, and great fun to be with. She seemed well educated — I felt she could come from any town or city in the United States. She showed excellent taste in decorating her little house, dressed herself and her children in the same manner, was interested in many more worldly subjects, and expertly ran the hotel. It wasn't until the last day of our visit there that she told me she had been born in the tiny village of Bettles, went to a missionary school there, and had never been farther south than Fairbanks.

With Hannah's return, Anne and I lost our bed, but two construction workers volunteered to double up so that we could move into a one-window, closetlike room upstairs. The only furniture was two cots, which Lowell and I used, putting Anne on a folding canvas camp bed between us. We hung our clothes on hooks, folded other items on a high shelf, put our books and alarm clock on the window sill, and felt right at home. The one drawback to our new quarters proved to be more amusing than difficult: the only exit from our room was through the recreation room where the men were living! And the walls were cardboard, so snorers and sleepwalkers were highly unpopular. J.P. was a constant offender, but the snoring prize went to one of the men way down the hall. We never did find out whether he was army or civilian. Fortunately we all considered ourselves one happy family at this stage of the expedition, so that the men paid no attention to my wanderings in and out. I found it hardest, though, to get used to sharing one bathroom with twenty men.

Actually, during most of the day Anne and I found ourselves alone in the big log house, while all the men were off working. When time began to drag, we started out to explore the base. Beyond the white, rectangular communications building next to us, and a garage and supply shed, we found a group of five two-story white houses clustered together. Little gardens and squares of grass between them. A dozen children were riding bicycles and pulling carts up and down the gravel paths. Anne made friends immediately and was off to some swings and seesaws with the whole gang, while I went in to have coffee with one of the mothers who had stuck her head out of the door upon our arrival. Each house was divided into two attractive, compact apartments, one upstairs and one down. They had big living rooms, a modern kitchen, three bedrooms, and a bath. Fortunately there were plenty of basements for the children to play in during the long dark winters. The sun, then, is up for only a few hours a day, and, as the welcome sign indicated, it is usually bitter cold outside. The summers begin about the middle of June, when the snow melts away, and end the middle of August when the first frost appears. Despite the rugged conditions, I never heard a word of complaint from any of the women. In fact, most were happy and enthusiastic about their life up there. Their husbands worked for the CAA for two years at a time, with a two-month paid vacation each year. Andy later told us that in one year the airlines sold 183 tickets to personnel leaving Bettles Field for various points in the states, five times the total population of the village. His records show that people traveled to such faraway places as Canton Island (in the Pacific), West Virginia, Minneapolis, Oklahoma City, and New Mexico.

I had many pleasant visits with the women while Anne played with her friends (the children, incidentally, looked healthier and more robust than many back home, despite the lack of sun and extreme cold). One wife, the only one who was an Eskimo, proudly showed me her magnificent fur parka, then astounded me by saying that not only had she sewed it herself but she had also trapped, skinned, and cured each of the thirty-three muskrat pelts!

While we were being social, the men were working hard, finding and filming the prospectors and Eskimos. On July 16th, they flew up into the hills to talk to a couple of old-time prospectors at Porcupine Creek. The two men had built an airstrip of sorts next to their camp, and Andy flew in once a month with mail and supplies — their only contact with the outside world.

The sixteenth also happened to be my birthday, something of very minor importance, to be sure. But, what with being so far from home and way off in the middle of nowhere, I felt horribly sorry for myself all day long because no one, including my husband, remembered my "special occasion." By seven that evening, when the two planes finally returned, buzzing the field in hair-raising military formation, I was in a most miserable state of being. Then Lowell jumped out of his plane, kissed me, said, "Happy birthday," and presented me with the prettiest bouquet of lavender arctic wild flowers. Lowell is a man who doesn't usually think of calling the florist back home, so that when he went out of his way to pick some flowers up at Porcupine Creek, I was floored!

Then he told me, most mysteriously, that I had to go along with him the next day to receive my birthday present. No amount of questioning persuaded him to say anything further. After dinner that night, the Andersons brought in a big cake with all the birthday trimmings, and everyone shared in the celebration. What a lovely birthday after such undeserving behavior!

The next day was a big and exciting one for all of us, in one way or another. We were out on the air strip at 8 A.M., checking over *Charlie* and loading camera equipment and a picnic lunch. Usually I take the less complicated checks — wing and tail surfaces, aileron hinges, propeller, flaps — while Lowell takes a look at the engine and drains the gas for signs of water. Today he had to cope with a last-minute camera problem, so I tried to do everything. I had trouble fastening the little engine access door on the cowling, but finally thought I'd closed it properly. Then we all climbed aboard and, to my usual consternation, Lowell and Merrill executed one of their simultaneous precision take-offs. (The two little planes flying wing to wing.) When two old-time military pilots get together! A few moments after take-off, Merrill started wiggling his wings, motioning frantically toward our engine, looking most concerned. (We had not tuned up our radio frequency yet.) Lowell instantly banked sharply, heading back for the field. My heart sank. Was it another oil leak, like the near-fatal one we had had over Africa, or a dreaded fire? We both checked all the instruments, but could find nothing amiss. We were down in a few more moments and Lowell leaped out, while Merrill circled overhead. You can imagine how I felt when he returned with a look of disgust — the engine access door had blown open. I was in the doghouse, and we were a good twenty minutes late.

Now it was Merrill's turn to delay our day. Both planes headed north and east, but we soon noticed that Merrill was flying farther and farther north. At first we thought he was trying for the usual short cut, but by the time they were almost out of sight, behind a line of hills, we knew that one of us was going the wrong way. We carefully rechecked our maps and headings and decided that Merrill was in for quite a surprise. Lowell could have radioed him, but decided to let matters rest — to be mean or funny, I don't know which.

A half hour's flight, and then lying against the far side of a big hill we found a long rectangular clearing. I just can't call it an air strip. It was too short and much too narrow, surrounded by trees and partly covered by tall grass, hummocks, and stones. We also had to land into that hill, so that I was a wreck by the time the brakes jerked us to a halt. We decided not to wait for Merrill, but parked the plane in the shrubbery and hiked off through the woods to the prospectors' home.

In a few hundred yards we came to a lovely clearing with a log cabin in the middle, a vegetable garden to the right, and a shed and food cache (a little house built on "stilts" about ten feet above the ground — to discourage any four-legged neighbors) on the left. A wire ran from the shed to the house, and tied to it were two of the most ferocious huskies we've ever seen. They snarled and bared their teeth as we came near. (We discovered, after we'd been there awhile, that the men passing by didn't bother them nearly as much as when Anne and I came near. One look at us and they went wild. I doubt that they had ever seen a white woman or child before. In fact, I doubt that the two prospectors had ever seen very many either.)

Oberon and Sam Stanish were two lean, leathery-faced brothers, both in their seventies, who had immigrated from Yugoslavia when they were in their teens. They had gone up to Alaska after a few years of working in a mine in Minnesota, staked a claim on Porcupine Creek, and have stayed right there ever since. They have an occasional visitor drop in by air; the bush pilot brings mail and supplies once a month, and they have a radio. That is the extent to which they are touched by the world outside.

They greeted us in front of their home, in clean shirts and blue jeans, obviously slicked up for my benefit. In halting English they told us about their garden, showed us the rows of lettuce, turnips, and cabbages. On one side of the house they had a little greenhouse, where they kept their tomato plants. (I doubt they could stay there during the winter.) Beside the doorway hung a Winchester frontier-type rifle, several pairs of snowshoes, and traps of various sizes. The house itself was made like most of the log ones we had already seen, with one door and four windows. Only instead of wood shingles on the roof, they had used sections of flattened gasoline tins, with sods just beneath, for insulation.

Going inside, we entered a large room, with a huge old black stove covering most of one side, bunks along another, and a table and chairs on the third wall. The wood floor had just been swept, the beds were made, and everything looked remarkably neat for bachelors' quarters. Anne was fascinated by the "wallpaper" — the walls were covered with old newspaper and magazine pictures, calendar girls, post cards, and so forth. That would keep her occupied for the next hour. That plus a chocolate bar that Sam gave her. We were served steaming mugs of coffee, and then I was presented with a small piece of folded newspaper. "Happy birthday," they both said, with their sweet, almost toothless smiles and strong accents. I carefully unwrapped it and found a small gold nugget. A birthday present I will long cherish!

By the time we were on our second cups of coffee, we heard Merrill's plane buzz over, and in a few moments in walked three sheepish men, resenting our roars of laughter. They had headed for another settlement (Wiseman) miles away, thinking we were the ones who were lost. I offered my services as a navigator, but that wasn't accepted too well either.

Time to start the day's filming — today would be the gold-panning sequence, a pastime I had been looking forward to watching ever since reaching Alaska. We hiked along Porcupine Creek for about half a mile (passing a woodpile to end all woodpiles — virtually a hundred yards long), scrambling over piles of rocks and boulders, the remainder of many years of digging in the creek. We had to cross and recross the little stream on narrow, makeshift bridges and planks. Such "tightrope walking" always frightens me, but Anne thought it great sport, insisting on edging herself across every one alone. I had visions of a very wet little girl being dried out in front of that big black stove, but no such ill luck, and we reached the workings long after the others.

The brothers have replaced the old panning method with a larger-scale operation, a sluice box. They built a slanting wooden trench in the middle of the stream; then, wearing hip boots, they shovel rocks from the stream bed into the upper part of the trench. Water, piped from above stream, washes the rocks down the trench, the lighter stones riding on top of a wooden grillwork, the heavier particles of gold falling beneath to the bottom of the trench. The unwanted stones are discarded at the water's edge, and every hour or so the men remove the wood grill to collect the pay dirt. They do find it, too — no one knows how much, but it's widely thought to be a wealthy claim. The brothers are supposed to be saving most of their gold, spending just enough for the bare essentials needed to live there. We heard many stories from local people of their reputed wealth, but one that was told us is probably more truth than fiction: when World War II broke out, the Stanishes flew down to Fairbanks and invested in $35,000 worth of war bonds!

Wealthy prospectors are rare, though. In fact, any sourdoughs like Sam and Oberon are unusual, even in Alaska. (I was intrigued with the word "sourdough" and its origin — the early Alaskan prospectors were called that because of the lump of sour dough they carried in their packs to bake bread while out in the bush.) Today many gold-seeking Alaskans pan in their spare time, or as a part-time occupation in the summer months. But as one old-timer put it, "A man could pan himself two dollars a day from the creek. He can make ten times that, washing dishes in town."

Oberon and Sam asked us if we would like to try our luck at gold panning and everybody accepted with great eagerness. Merrill spent most of the morning working at it, hoping for a nugget for his fiancée (he found one big enough for her charm bracelet). J.P. and Mike each took only one turn, found pieces so tiny they had to keep them between layers of Scotch tape. I tried, too, but not for long — it is very hard work! We had to stand on slippery rocks in the middle of the stream, plunge our hands into water that was so cold I could hardly take it for more than a few minutes at a time, and continually swirl the stones and sand back and forth, round and round. We gradually dumped out the upper layers of debris, and if we were lucky, we finally found a particle or two of dull gold at the bottom of the empty pan.

Anne thought this odd "game" great sport and joined in with the greatest of gusto (water, pots, and pans are her greatest joy in life), but she had no interest in the object of our search. It was the swirling water that fascinated her, and she proceeded to get herself so wet that we had to get back to that big black stove after all.

Then it was good-by to our friends the Stanishes and back to Bettles after what felt like a fascinating glimpse into Alaska's past. The next day, July 18th, we had another look into her past, an experience which was in many ways the highlight of our whole trip. Lowell had spent weeks of research on Alaskan Eskimos and had made many inquiries as to where we might find a group which was still relatively untouched by Western civilization. We knew beforehand that this would be difficult because most Eskimos these days look and live just about like anybody else in the United States — instead of an igloo, it's a house; the children go to school, wear blue jeans, dance the rock and roll; the mothers run their households about the same way we do, and the fathers have similar jobs.

The Eskimos in Alaska number about 16,000, living mostly in the extreme north and northwest, in towns such as Barrow and Kotzebue, and other villages along the Arctic Ocean and Bering Sea. Hunting is still a chief occupation — the caribou or whale and walrus. But they hunt with the latest-model rifles (perhaps with sunglasses to help the eyes), and their boats are powered by the latest-model outboard motors.

Tourism provides an occupation for many: the making of Eskimo artifacts and the staging of dances and hunts. But the Eskimo has also become wise to that weird breed of American, the tourist, and prices are scaled accordingly.

Many Eskimo men work for the Dew Line, where no racial discrimination is found. The Eskimos are phenomenal mechanics and are considered among the best workers in this field. They also make excellent pilots, and several are flying for Wein today. Others are making brilliant careers for themselves as teachers, labor leaders, and members of the State Legislature. And it probably won't be too long before an Eskimo congressman or senator will be representing his state in Washington.

We did learn of a nomadic group living deep in the Brooks Mountain range, who were probably the least affected by "white man's ways." We also found that there was no air strip or field, or even sand bar nearby for *Charlie* to land on. In fact, the closest we could get was Bettles. These people, fifteen or twenty families, lived in Anaktuvuk Pass and their only contact with the outside world was, like the prospectors, the bush pilot. In this case, it had to be a seaplane that landed on a small lake a mile or so from their homes.

Early on the morning of the eighteenth, Mike, J.P., and Bill flew up to the pass with Andy, and when Andy returned two hours later, Merrill flew the three of us up. (We couldn't get over how versatile Merrill was — big planes, little planes, wheels, skis, and now pontoons!) We rode in a jeep to a nearby river and then climbed down a ladder to a small dock. The Cessna 180, on floats, was waiting there, and we all clambered aboard, Anne and I sharing a little canvaslike seat in the rear.

Taking off on the water for a change was great fun, with the spray splashing against our side windows. But when I caught a glimpse, through the sheets of water, of the river-bank rising just ahead of us, while we were still "down," I went into another grand panic. Then, at the last moment, it seemed, Merrill swung the plane to the right. We rounded the river bend on one pontoon and then took off on the stretch of straight water just ahead of us.

Once off, we turned north toward the Brooks Mountains, following the John River (a branch of the Koyukuk) as it wound its way through them. As usual, we flew a bare few hundred feet above the ground and, as usual, flew in and out of several rain showers. (At home, when we fly through rain-storms, we invariably encounter very poor visibility and most often dodge around them. Here in Alaska, the visibility in the frequent rain was seldom less than five to ten miles, and often even more. Perhaps it is because the atmosphere there has so little city pollution. So, of course, we never thought much of encountering rain, even in the mountains.)

How different these mountains were from those farther south — a series of low, smoothly rounded green humps — no snow-covered peaks or rocky precipices, no trees even. Heavy snow covering for ten months of the year has worn the con-tours smooth, and nothing but the tundra can grow here, where the permafrost lies just beneath the surface of the ground.

The ground rose higher and higher beneath us until it seemed we were just skimming above it. Now we were almost through the mountains and in the wide, flat Anaktuvuk Pass. I was thrilled to think that only 150 miles of flat tundra now lay between us and the Arctic coastline, and beyond that, one thousand miles farther over the ice, was the North Pole.

We had been aware of what looked like piles of white sticks beneath us, and now we finally realized that they were caribou bones and antlers. The floor of the pass was dotted with these relics — a virtual graveyard. Herds of thousands of caribou migrate through these mountains twice a year, and this is their main route. They pour down between the mountain walls in an almost never-ending wide stream, and the Eskimos and wolves make big inroads into such confusion. I imagine a good many succumb to natural causes, too.

Then we zoomed over the rooftops of our first Eskimo settlement, a dozen boxlike wood houses on the south side of the small lake, a trading post, and a small log church. Five minutes later Merrill banked steeply over a second lake, buzzing so low over three more homes that if they'd had a second story we would have hit it. We were down on the lake within a few moments, and Merrill pushed the pontoons up among the tundra bushes at the water's edge.

A young Eskimo boy was waiting and greeted us with a big smile and, "Hello, my name is John. You'd better follow me up to our home." The good English we expected — but when we later discovered that John and his brother were the only two among the three families that could really speak it, we were surprised. (The boys received their schooling from a missionary school near Bettles.)

The Eskimo homes appeared to be about half a mile away, a mere stroll if we were on a road, an exhausting struggle across the soggy tundra. In the summertime the soil surface melts, but the ground just beneath remains frozen, so that the result is a virtual lake of water and mud beneath the green tundra bushes. The trick was to try to tightrope walk along the higher mounds of earth, struggling to avoid the low spots where we would sink in above our ankles. We wore rubbers, but they did no good at all — it was boots that we really needed or, better yet, a boat! The only one who enjoyed the nightmarish walk was Anne, as usual, ridding pig-a-back on her daddy's shoulders.

At times, when the going was less difficult, we could pause to look for the lovely wild flowers half-hidden among the green thickets. We were amazed at how exquisite and colorful they were, and how abundant. Occasionally we had to jump over a little stream, and here we often found chunks of ice half-hidden by the turf. The Eskimos told us later that they used these little ice-filled niches for summertime refrigerators — storing meat there from May until September.

There were other signs of the winter past — occasional patches of ice and snow lying in a shady spot at the foot of a mountain or along the edge of a stream. But that was all — the rest of the countryside was a blend of greens and browns unbroken by rocks or trees, or by vivid colors or irregular shapes (except for the little brown huts just ahead of us) — just gentle smooth contours of the softly muted landscape. How still it was, too. We were not conscious of any sound, even wind or birds. I have heard that the common adjectives used for this area are barren, forbidding wastes, but we were both agreed that it appealed to us more than almost any place we had yet seen. Perhaps because of the infinitely peaceful, out-of-this-world-like atmosphere of which we were both so greatly aware.

The silence was shattered by the barking of dogs as we drew nearer to the Eskimo homes. In fact we were practically

overwhelmed by dogs — big ones and countless bouncing
puppies. No magnificent huskies like our friends the prospectors owned, but mongrels of all sizes and colors. Anne was
thrilled—no need to worry about viciousness—they all wanted
to play with her.

We were in front of the first of three little houses — one-
room homes made of lumber undoubtedly flown in by bush
pilots. The first house (or *wykiup*, as the Eskimos call
them) had several small glass windows, a canvas roof, and sod
covering the bottom half of the plain wood walls. In the
wintertime, we were told, these rectangular blocks of mud
cover the entire home, including the roof — almost foolproof
protection against the snow and cold. Unfortunately, the
general conception that Eskimos in Alaska live in ice igloos
is a mistake. Igloos are found only among the nomadic Eskimos of the Canadian Far North.

The only jarring notes to the attractive surroundings were
the large mud- and water-filled holes, from which the Eskimos
took the sod, covering most of the ground around the houses.
The miserable mudholes also appeared to serve as garbage
receptacles and undoubtedly were welcome areas for mosquito
breeding.

Of the latter, there were more than enough to spare. We had
been amply forewarned about the gigantic Alaskan mosquito,
but until then we had had surprisingly few encounters with
them. We had taken a new repellent with us, one which Alaskans now swear by, and until then it had been a great success.
That morning we had all practically bathed in it. We smelled
terribly, and fortunately the mosquitoes thought so, too.
Clouds of them swarmed about us, but never dared alight.
We were told that the Eskimos had heard about "Off," too,
and the bush pilots had standing orders for a number of bottles
every month.

When we reached the door of the first house, a young Eskimo man came out to greet us in flawless English. His name was Abraham, and our little boy guide was his brother. We gathered that three large families lived in the three houses, but the relationships were all most confusing to me. At that moment an older man, Simon, with a young boy and a dog, walked up. They were just returning from hunting. Simon carried a gun and the dog had what looked like saddlebags hung over his back. We assumed that the hunt hadn't been too successful because the bags looked quite empty. Ducks or smaller animals like rabbits were the prey this time. But any day now the huge caribou herds were due to migrate through this pass and these hunters would have a busy time. Plenty of meat was needed for the long winter ahead.

The two men invited us inside their home, and we gladly accepted. It was windy and cold, and I felt thoroughly chilled. Inside it was warm and dark and clean and orderly. As our eyes grew accustomed to the dimness, we could see members of the household eyeing us quietly from the shadows. The one woman looked like the mother of the two boys, and a third little boy was staring at us from a far corner. His name was Franklin Roosevelt. (The other names were undoubtedly a result of the work of the missionaires — the Democrats must have sneaked in here!) His father or grandfather, I'm not sure which, proudly told us that he was almost three years old, just Anne's age. I hoped that he and Anne might play together during the day, but little Franklin was very shy and Anne was almost as bad, for a change. So they both just stood and eyed each other, thumbs in mouths. Anne was a good foot taller and more solidly built, but then she is bigger than most of her playmates back home.

We all sat on wooden benches which lined two walls. A

black potbellied stove stood in the middle of the room, a few pots and pans and eating utensils on the floor beside it. The rest of the room was quite bare, except for numerous parkas and furs hanging from the pegs on the walls. I gathered that the big skins (caribou, I think) were used for bedding at night. Lowell talked with the young man a bit, while the rest of us just sat. Then he asked if we might eat our picnic lunch inside. They said, of course, graciously, but would not join us, either by accepting our offer of sandwiches or cooking anything for themselves. I am afraid that if we really wanted to become friends with this family we would have to come prepared to live there for a while. If we only had the time, how I'd love such an interlude.

One amusing incident helped break the complete silence at lunchtime — leave it to the children! A screen curtain hung across the doorway, a good protection against the mosquitoes, and when we all went inside, one overly friendly little puppy tried to follow. This was obviously not allowed, because the father shoved him right back out. But he was a persistent little pup and squeezed right back in again and again, usually waiting until the grownups were occupied with something else. The children, including Anne, would all start to giggle as the little imp wiggled his way in. When the giggles turned to shouts of laughter, the father usually gathered something was up, and out went the little puppy again. I don't know who was having the most fun, but I suspect it may have been the father.

When lunch was over, we all trooped over to a second *wykiup*, past an incongruous-looking sled sitting on the mud. This was the home of Elijah, brother of Simon. He was an older man, with little steel-rimmed glasses sitting on the end of his nose. The other men had worn western-style jackets and pants, but Elijah wore the traditional warm-weather Eskimo parka — of cloth, with wolverine fur around the hood. We wondered why the fur, which hid most of his face, and we finally decided that it was good protection against the pesky mosquitoes. All the men wore Eskimo boots of leather, completely waterproof, an item we envied. Their women sew the caribou leather together with thongs which expand when becoming wet.

Elijah's wife came to the doorway, a lovely white-haired woman who also wore glasses, and her parka had the latest "flapper" look. It was shapeless, hung to her boots, and was of a bright orange and yellow flowered material. I am sure she spent many hours making it and was rightly proud of it.

Her home was similar to the first inside, but more cluttered with belongings. They had built-in bunks in two corners of the room, with gay flowered curtains draped around them. The usual black stove was in the center, with a table by it this time and a Singer sewing machine sitting proudly on top of it. I also noticed a good pair of binoculars hanging from a peg on the wall. Next to it hung two painted face masks of wood, with wolverine fringes. When we inquired about these unusual artifices, Elijah said that he was making them and sending them out by bush pilots to sell to tourists farther south. (In the early days masks were used in Eskimo ritual dances.) He carved the faces out of wood with a sharp knife, adding hair and eyebrows of wolf's fur, copying the image he saw in a mirror. We bought one of the masks from him and now realize that it looks exactly like our friend Elijah!

Elijah asked if we would like to see the baby (again I was completely confused by relationships, probably his grandchild) and drew aside the curtains of one bed. A tiny infant was sleeping there, with his mother sitting beside him. She was a plump, smiling young woman who could speak no English, and the baby was adorable, about six months old, wearing a black flowered dress and knitted booties. She never awakened while we were there, even when we turned our bright camera lights right on her face.

We also filmed old Mrs. Elijah using her sewing machine, and we got a good surprise (and picture) when she paused to pick up an ivory cigarette holder, put a homemade cigarette in it, and nonchalantly puffed away.

The highlight of the visit, for Anne, came when Elijah took us out to see the wolf puppies they had just captured. Apparently the mother had been killed or died, and these Eskimos found the four pups in a little cave. They were being kept there in a cage until a bush pilot could fly them out, sending them on their way to the zoo. In return, the Eskimos were to be paid well for such a find. We gathered that they never tried to tame wolves, that here was an animal that one couldn't domesticate. We found this very hard to believe when playing with the friendly little pups. They had soft black hair, little pink noses and tongues, and looked just like dogs in almost every respect. The moment they started running, though, we knew they were wolves — they had that distinctive slinking lope. Anne and little Franklin Roosevelt cuddled them and chased them about, almost breaking the ice between them with a few tentative smiles and children's meaningful looks. It would not have taken long, as language is a small barrier between little ones.

All too soon it was time for us to leave. Since we had to make two trips, it would be four more hours before the last of the men could finally reach Bettles. Anne and I went first, with Bill Bouchat, struggling through the tundra once again to the plane tied to a bush at the lake's edge. Elijah came with us and we watched him throw a small fish net into the water, trying to catch some arctic graylings for dinner that night. We finally climbed aboard, and Merrill applied power. Nothing happened — more power, with rocking motions. Merrill looked terribly concerned. He glanced over his shoulder and then erupted with unprintable language. We looked past him, as he leaped out the door, and saw Lowell, J.P., and Mike with broad grins, and a stout rope still holding the pontoons to the shore. Great joke! Just one of the many constantly being pulled on Merrill. They were always ribbing and kidding him, perhaps because he is so serious and yet good-natured. He never knew when he walked out to his plane on the day of a flight just what added attraction he might find. One time a number of film reels were hanging from the aerial, and another day his entire door had been removed. But the greatest torment for him was the time he came out to the plane to find J.P. and Mike looking at the engine through the cowling access door. When he appeared, they glanced at each other and then quickly closed the door. He was left to wonder during the entire flight just what had been going on with the engine! Lowell's greatest triumph came during the week of the 4th of July. Firecrackers had been plentiful in Alaska and we all did our share of making some noise. Lowell found some fake ones at a roadside stand and one morning, when the men were slow about waking, he sneaked into their room and tossed this realistic fake with a lighted wick right at the foot of their beds. He said he had never seen four men leap up and leave a room faster. Irrevocable damage was done to dispositions that day.

So the jokesters were finally persuaded to untie the rope and we were on our way, with another hair-raising take-off. The lake was small and we had a good load. Merrill jerked his flaps down when we were about halfway down the lake, then began "rocking" to help ease it from the water. The pontoons slipped over the tundra just a few feet up. Routine for bush pilots, I am sure. It's just that I haven't got what it takes to be a bush pilot!

This was a sad flight for us in a way — it drew the curtain on our Arctic adventure. Anne was asleep on the seat beside me as I watched the quiet tundra hills slip away beneath us. Before the whole journey began, I remembered my great misgivings and feelings of guilt at forcing a little one like Anne out of a normal home environment into a life so strenuous and unsettled. Now I knew that I was wrong, that Anne adjusts even better than we, and I am sure she was far happier being with us, wherever we were, than at home with us away. Now I could hardly wait to return home and make plans for the next expedition with both children!

Our Alaskan odyssey was most successful in other ways, too. Lowell, J.P., and Mike had obtained what they wanted in the way of film and, in the process, had proved to themselves and to the rest of the industry that a good film story could be made on a simple scale with a three-man crew rather than an elaborate production with many people involved. And we had discovered for ourselves that, while we had always felt that a husband-and-wife combination was the perfect size for an expedition, it was just as much fun to join up with a small group, too. We felt very fortunate to have found such a perfect team. Never once, even under the most adverse conditions, did either of us ever hear a grumble. Rather, everyone was always ready for more humor and eager for whatever else might come.

But the most important achievement of the whole trip for us — with *Charlie's* help we followed the North Star from the awesome mountains and glaciers of southern Alaska to the endless tundra of the Arctic and, in the process, gained a little firsthand knowledge of our rugged new state and a great enthusiasm for what we found. We loved the people, their towns and cities, their way of life, the magnificent countryside, the whole atmosphere of rugged outdoor living, friendliness, and incentive. In fact, we were so sold on our forty-ninth state that we often talk of moving up there to live, and we know Anne would be the first to agree!

1